Being Jewish
After the Destruction
of Gaza

Being Jewish After the Destruction of Gaza

A Reckoning

Peter Beinart

ALFRED A. KNOPF · New York

2025

THIS IS A BORZOI BOOK
PUBLISHED BY ALFRED A. KNOPF

www.aaknopf.com

Knopf, Borzoi Books, and the colophon are registered
trademarks of Penguin Random House LLC.

Library of Congress Cataloging-in-Publication Data
Names: Beinart, Peter, author.
Title: Being Jewish after the destruction of Gaza :
a reckoning / Peter Beinart.
Description: First edition. | New York : Alfred A. Knopf, [2025] |
This is a Borzoi book. | Includes bibliographical references.
Identifiers: LCCN 2024039692 | ISBN 9780593803899 (hardcover) |
ISBN 9780593803905 (ebook)
Subjects: LCSH: October 7 Hamas Attack, 2023—Influence. |
Israel-Hamas War, 2023—Influence. |Jews—Identity. | Palestinian
Arabs—Relations—Israel. | Israel—Relations—Palestinian Arab.
Classification: LCC DS119.77 .B45 2025 |
DDC 956.9405/5—dc23/eng/20240906
LC record available at https://lccn.loc.gov/2024039692

Jacket background image by Roland Kraemer/Stocksy/Adobe Stock
Jacket design by Madeline Partner

Manufactured in the United States of America
First Edition

In memory of my grandmother Adele Pienaar, z"l.
She disagreed with the arguments in this book.
And her spirit is on every page.

Judaism is about the universality of justice but the particularity of love.

—RABBI JONATHAN SACKS

Contents

Being Jewish
After the Destruction
of Gaza

A Note to My Former Friend

I think about you often, and about the argument that has divided us. I know you believe that my public opposition to this war—and to the very idea of a state that favors Jews over Palestinians—constitutes a betrayal of our people. I know you think I am putting your family at risk.

The breach in our relationship mirrors a broader schism within our tribe, between Americans and Israelis, left and right, young and old. When I enter a synagogue, I am no longer sure who will extend their hand and who will look away. Maybe you feel a similar anxiety in progressive circles where you once felt at home. Jews have always quarreled, and we should. But I worry that given the trajectory of events in Israel and Palestine, we may be moving past mere disagreement, toward hatred.

I don't want to add to that rancor and pain. While I hope to persuade you of my views, our tradition insists that I have obligations to you whether I convince you or not. And it offers models for how to express those obligations. When I think about the relationship I seek, two such models come to mind.

In the first, I—and those Jews who agree with me—am

Elisha Ben Abuya and you are Rabbi Meir. The Talmud calls Elisha a heretic. Some say he lost his faith when he witnessed a boy obey his father's request to perform a mitzvah and then die. Others say it happened when he saw the tongue of a murdered sage lying in the street. Either way, most rabbis would not even utter his name. They said that when he lay in the womb, apostasy flowed through his mother like the "poison of a snake." They called him *acher,* Other, the one beyond the pale.

But not his former student Rabbi Meir. One Shabbat, Elisha passed Rabbi Meir's study hall while riding a horse, an act prohibited on the day of rest. Nonetheless, Rabbi Meir cut short his lecture and began walking alongside the notorious rebel. The two discussed Torah until Elisha warned Rabbi Meir that if he ventured farther, he would violate the two thousand cubits he was permitted to walk on Shabbat. Elisha continued on—past boundaries that Rabbi Meir would not cross—just as I have crossed boundaries that you will not cross in my views about Israel and Palestine. But they walked as far as they could together and parted with respect.

In the second model, I—and my ilk—am David Malter and you are Rabbi Isaac Saunders in Chaim Potok's novel *The Chosen.* In 1940s Brooklyn, the two clash ferociously over the creation of a Jewish state. Yet when Malter's son says he hates Saunders, Malter defends his ideological rival. He says it is "the faith of Jews like Reb Saunders" that has "kept us alive through two thousand years of violent persecution."

The debate about Israel has changed radically since then. Yet your fervent nationalism reminds me of Reb Saunders's fervent faith. It frightens and comforts me at the same time.

I consider your single-minded focus on Israeli security to be immoral and self-defeating. It justifies actions that I consider grave crimes. It blinds you to the essential interconnectedness of Jewish and Palestinian safety. When I hear you thunder about the Israelis murdered and captured on October 7, I wish you would summon some of that righteous anger for the Palestinians slaughtered in even greater numbers. That's why I titled this book *Being Jewish After the Destruction of Gaza,* not *Being Jewish After October 7.* It's not because I minimize that day. Like you, I remain shaken by its horror. I chose the former as a title because I know you grapple with the terror of that day. I worry that you don't grapple sufficiently with the terror of the days that followed, and preceded it, as well.

I see you as David Malter saw Reb Saunders, as a kind of fanatic. But there is a part of me that suspects it is your fanaticism, like his, that has sustained our people in a pitiless world. When I see you wearing dog tags to remind yourself, every hour of every day, of the hostages in Gaza, I know that if I were among those hostages, you would fight obsessively for my release. You would do so precisely because of the tribalism I fear. And in my nightmares, I imagine myself— abandoned by all the enlightened universalists—knocking anxiously at your door.

By reading these words, you have agreed to walk with me. I hope to lure you beyond established boundaries. But wherever we part, I hope the rupture is not final, that our journey together is not done.

Prologue: We Need a New Story

The Talmud poses a question: If you steal from a Jew who dies with no living relatives, how do you pay back the money? It then dismisses the premise: No Jew is without relatives. As the famed medieval commentator Rashi explains, we are all children of our forefather Jacob. We are all each other's relatives.

That's how I was raised to see the world: Jews are an extended family. I didn't learn the notion primarily from sacred texts. I absorbed it—via a thousand stray comments— from the Jews who raised me.

I remember walking as a child with my grandfather into an apartment building in a heavily Jewish suburb of Boston. Despite living in South Africa and having only the dimmest acquaintance with the area, he seemed entirely at ease. When I saw him inspecting names next to the doorbell, I asked if he knew any of these people. He said he knew them all.

When I was preparing to leave for college, I noticed my mother doing the same thing. She was anxious. We had barely any American relatives; it had always been just the four of us. Now I, the oldest child, was departing. We had received an envelope with information about my campus housing. She scanned the list of students in my dorm and began reciting the familiar ones aloud: Shapiro, Spector, Klein. It was her way of reassuring herself that I would not be alone.

I rolled my eyes back then. But this way of perceiving the world sank in. Many decades later, I was at a conference in Colorado when I learned my grandmother had died. It was Friday and I couldn't fly to Cape Town until Shabbat ended. I went to the local Chabad, watched the rabbi's children run wild—as I once did at my grandmother's Shabbat meals— talked to strangers until late into the night, and knew she would be happy, because I was with family.

How does someone like me, who still considers himself a Jewish loyalist, end up being cursed on the street by people who believe Jewish loyalty requires my excommunication? It began at those very Shabbat meals in Cape Town, when I began considering the other people who were present. They hovered around the periphery, in the kitchen or the garden, doing the menial work. They were legally subordinate, which, I was told, was necessary. Because they would kill us if they could. Somewhere, their Black terror army was plotting to do just that.

As I reached adulthood, that story collapsed. Apartheid ended. The army that had frightened so many whites disbanded once Black South Africans could express themselves with a ballot rather than a gun. Profound inequities remained; the country did not live happily ever after. Still, the story I heard constantly in my youth—that safety required supremacy—largely disappeared. It's now an embarrassment. Barely anyone tells that story about South Africa anymore.

Yet every day, Jews tell it about Israel. I hear it from people I know, respect, even love. It's as if Jews from around the world were seated together, in a single house, for Shabbat. Some of us live there; others are visiting. Time slows as night falls. You can almost hear everyone exhale. I want to be at that table, a member in good standing, because the house is in a place we have always considered precious. And because it's home to almost half the Jews on earth.

But other people lived there before the house was even built. For a long time, they've been crowded into cramped, squalid rooms. Now their condition has grown even more dire. Some are malnourished; many are screaming in pain. Some people at the table claim the screams are contrived and the wounds are fake. Others acknowledge that the injuries are real but insist that these unfortunates brought the suffering upon themselves. They've committed unspeakable crimes. They want us dead. We have no choice.

This book is about the story Jews tell ourselves to block out the screams. It's about the story that enables our leaders, our families, and our friends to watch the destruction of the Gaza Strip—the flattening of universities, the people forced to make bread from hay, the children freezing to death under buildings turned to rubble by a state that speaks in our name—and shrug, if not applaud. It's about the story that convinces even Jews who are genuinely pained by Gaza's agony that there is no other way to keep us safe. It's our version of a story told in many variations by many peoples in many places who decide that protecting themselves requires subjugating others, that equality is tantamount to death.

My hope is that we will one day see Gaza's obliteration as

a turning point in Jewish history. From the destruction of the Second Temple to the expulsion from Spain to the Holocaust, Jews have told new stories to answer the horrors we endured. We must now tell a new story to answer the horror that a Jewish country has perpetrated, with the support of many Jews around the world. Its central element should be this: We are not history's permanent virtuous victims. We are not hardwired to forever endure evil but never commit it. That false innocence, which pervades contemporary Jewish life, camouflages domination as self-defense. It exempts Jews from external judgment. It offers infinite license to fallible human beings.

I still believe in the metaphor of Jews as a family. But it has been corrupted. Jewish leaders have turned our commitment to one another into a moral sedative. They have traded on our solidarity to justify starvation and slaughter. They have told us that the way to show we care about the Israelis taken hostage by Hamas is to support a war that kills and starves those very hostages, and that the way to honor the memory of the Israelis Hamas murdered is to support a war that will create tens of thousands more scarred, desperate young Palestinians eager to avenge their loved ones by taking Israeli lives. We need a new story—based on equality rather than supremacy—because the current one doesn't endanger only Palestinians. It endangers us.

This book is for the Jews who are still sitting at that Shabbat table, and for the Jews—sometimes their own children—who have left in disgust. I yearn for us to sit together. But not this way. Not as masters of the house.

1

They Tried to Kill Us, We Survived, Let's Eat

Every year, on the holiday of Purim, Jews dress in silly costumes, eat triangular pastries, and listen to an ancient story about attempted genocide. It comes from the book of Esther. The tale begins with a dissolute Persian king. He hosts a banquet, gets drunk, orders his queen to "display her beauty" to the revelers, and, when she refuses, banishes her from the throne. As her replacement he chooses Esther, a beautiful young maiden who, unbeknownst to him, is a Jew. Then he makes a calamitous personnel decision: He selects Haman, a pathological Jew-hater, to be his right-hand man. The stage is now set for an epic clash.

Haman persuades the king to sign an edict exterminating the Jews. Esther's uncle, Mordechai, hears the news and sends word that she must save her people. Although protesting puts her own life at risk, Esther appeals to the king and, through a series of daring maneuvers, turns him against Haman. Haman is hanged. Mordechai takes his job. Good triumphs over evil.

When we tell the story of Purim today, many of us stop

there. But that's not quite right. The book of Esther doesn't end with Haman's death. It continues because although Haman is gone, his edict to kill the Jews remains. The king can't reverse it. What he can do is empower Mordechai and his kinsmen to take matters into their own hands. Which they do. "The Jews struck at their enemies with the sword," proclaims the book of Esther, "slaying and destroying; they wreaked their will upon their enemies." On the thirteenth day of the month of Adar, the Jews kill seventy-five thousand people. They make the fourteenth "a day of feasting and merrymaking." With the blood of their foes barely dry, the Jews feast and make merry. That's the origin of Purim.

Purim isn't only about the danger gentiles pose to us. It's also about the danger we pose to them.

For most of our history, when Jews had little capacity to impose our will via the sword, the conclusion of the book of Esther was a harmless and even understandable fantasy. Who can blame a tormented people for dreaming of a world turned upside down? But the ending reads differently when Jews wield life-and-death power over millions of Palestinians who lack even a passport. Today, these blood-soaked verses should unsettle us. When we recite them aloud in synagogue, we should employ the anguished, sorrowful tune in which we chant the book of Lamentations, which depicts the destruction of our ancient temples.

Instead, most of us ignore the violence that concludes the Esther scroll. Some contemporary Jews justify it as self-defense. On the far right, some revel in it. But they're the exception. More often, we look away. We focus on what they tried to do to us. There's a joke that every Jewish holiday has the same plot: "They tried to kill us, we survived, let's eat." That's how many Jews narrate not only Purim but many of our other best-loved holidays. Passover recounts our liberation from bondage in Egypt. Chanukah celebrates the Maccabees, who freed us from persecution by the Syrian-Greek emperor Antiochus.

Festivals we can't fit into this script tend not to capture our collective imagination. Why is Shavuot, which commemorates the giving of the Torah, less well-known among contemporary Jews than Purim and Chanukah, holidays of lesser religious significance? There are various reasons: American Jews like Chanukah because it's our answer to Christmas; Israeli Jews like Chanukah because they've made it a proto-Zionist story of regained sovereignty; everyone likes Purim because it involves costumes. But there's one more explanation: Shavuot no longer fits the story we tell about ourselves. In modernity, Jews have grown more secular. Except for a religiously observant minority, we no longer describe ourselves as a people chosen by God to follow laws engraved at Sinai. We instead describe ourselves as a people fated by history to perpetually face annihilation but, miraculously, to survive.

With this secularization has come moral evasion. When explicating Jewish suffering, the rabbinic tradition relentlessly demands that Jews look inward and reckon with our sins. The Talmud blames the Jews for Haman's rise because we participated in the king's drunken debauchery. A midrash on the Song of Songs suggests that the Israelites enslaved in Egypt were unworthy of freedom because we worshipped idols. The Talmud devotes almost an entire tractate to how

Jews should respond to drought. Its answer: fast and repent for our misdeeds.

This theology is hard to stomach. When it is applied to modern calamities like the Holocaust, most Jews rightly consider any suggestion that we blame ourselves to be obscene. But in the absence of a belief in divine reward and punishment, we no longer wrestle in the same way with what our sacred texts say about Jewish ethical responsibility. Too often, we turn them into tales of Jewish innocence.

We've lost sight of our holidays' moral complexity. We generally end the story of Chanukah when the Maccabees defeat the Greeks and rededicate the Temple. But the Maccabees didn't disappear. They became the Hasmonean dynasty, which the rabbis of the Talmud disdained for amassing unchecked power and subverting the rule of law. We leave that part out.

When telling the Passover story, many American Jews emphasize the holiday's universal themes of tyranny and freedom. We acknowledge that other peoples endured bondage too. Lurking in the biblical text, however, is a more subversive message: not just that gentiles can be oppressed, but that Jews can be oppressors. Contemporary scholars note a remarkable inversion. In language strikingly similar to that used by the book of Exodus to describe Egyptian slavery, the book of Genesis describes how our patriarch and matriarch, Abraham and Sarah, enslaved a woman named Hagar, who according to one rabbinic tradition was Pharaoh's daughter. You rarely hear this at Passover seders, but according to the Bible, our ancestors were slaves and slaveholders too.

"They tried to kill us, we survived, let's eat" isn't the story of our festivals. It's a choice about what to see, and what not to see, in Judaism, and in ourselves. It imagines us as virtuous victims who survive great horrors. And then it brings down the curtain, until the show begins again.

I understand this narrative's power for our still-scarred people. My maternal grandmother traced her ancestry to northeastern Spain, from which Jews were expelled in the fifteenth century. Her mother was born in Rhodes, a Mediterranean island she was fortunate enough to leave before the Nazis deported its Jews to Auschwitz. My grandmother herself was born in Egypt but left as a child as antisemitism grew. She reminded me of these experiences when I expressed faith in America. She strongly advised me not to take Jewish safety for granted.

Many Jewish families project these personal histories onto our holidays. Mizrachi Jews, when reading about the Israelites who fled Pharaoh's Egypt without waiting for the dough to rise, sometimes recall their grandparents' hasty departure from Morocco, Yemen, or Iraq in the late 1940s and early 1950s. Many Ashkenazi Jews were raised on memories of the latter-day Pharaohs, Antiochuses, and Hamans, who in the nineteenth and twentieth centuries spilled Jewish blood like water in the lands between the Black and the Baltic Seas. Some have older relatives who chanted the Haggadah's famous refrain, "We were once slaves to Pharaoh in Egypt, now we are free," on the first Passover after being liberated from Bergen-Belsen or Majdanek. This is not ancient history. Within the lifetime of some older Jews, European Jewry was largely wiped out. There are still fewer Jews alive today than there were in 1939.

It's not surprising, then, that victim often feels like our natural role. But it's also a costume that our community urges upon us and re-tailors for the specifications of the moment. It evokes something familiar while concealing something unnerving, something our tradition knows: that Jews can be Pharaohs too.

This selective vision pervades contemporary Jewish life. Consider the way establishment Jewish groups invoke the Bible to validate the Jewish people's relationship to the land of Israel. In February 2024, the American Jewish Committee set out to rebut the claim that Israel is a settler-colonial state. To prove the Jewish connection to the land, it cites the book of Genesis, in which—as the AJC describes it—"God promises the land of Israel to Abraham, the first Jew." It then moves to the book of Exodus, in which "Moses leads the Israelites out of slavery and oppression in Egypt with a promise to take them back to the land of Israel, the land of their forefathers." Then it jumps ahead to the "books of Judges and Kings," which "relate the stories of Jewish rulers over the land of Israel."

People familiar with the Hebrew Bible will note a glaring omission: the book of Joshua, which explains how those Jewish rulers became rulers in the first place. According to the text, the Israelites under the leadership of Joshua Ben Nun conquered Canaan from the seven nations that lived there. The AJC's chronology skips over that.

One might reasonably ask: Who cares? The Bible is a religious document, not a historical one. No one knows whether Joshua Ben Nun actually conquered the territory or existed at all. And whether he did or not, it doesn't change the fact that Jews have an ancient and profound spiritual connection to this patch of land.

So then why does the AJC ignore the Bible's account of Joshua's invasion? Because it contradicts our contemporary narrative of victimhood. The only conquests the organization acknowledges are ones that come at the Jews' expense. "The Jewish people are indigenous to the land of Israel and first achieved self-determination there 3,000 years ago," declares the AJC, without ever explaining how that "self-determination" came to be. Then "the Romans expelled the majority of Jews in 70 C.E."

For groups like the AJC, which want to prove that Zionism isn't a colonial movement, the book of Joshua is inconvenient since, to contemporary ears, it sounds quite colonial itself. But that's one reason the early Zionists loved it. In his 1923 essay, "The Iron Wall," Vladimir Jabotinsky, the ideological forefather of the Israeli prime minister Benjamin Netanyahu's Likud Party, declared that in seizing Canaan, "our own ancestors under Joshua Ben Nun, behaved like brigands." He didn't mean that as a criticism. In 1948, the newly formed Israel Defense Forces named one of its key battles in Israel's war of independence Operation Ben-Nun. David Ben-Gurion, Israel's first prime minister, was obsessed with the biblical conqueror. In 1958 he hosted a bimonthly study group on the book of Joshua to which he invited luminaries of the young state.

Early Zionists embraced the tale of Joshua's conquest because they lived in an age of colonization when indigeneity wasn't a trump card. If you wanted the land, and believed you hailed from a more advanced civilization and could thus cultivate it better than the natives, that was justification enough. In 1902, Theodor Herzl, the founder of political Zionism, wrote to Cecil Rhodes, the arch-imperialist of southern Africa, and urged him to support Zionism "because it is something colonial." In "The Iron Wall," Jabotinsky called the Arabs of Mandatory Palestine "natives," whom he compared to the Sioux Indians. He called his fellow Zionists "colonists," who resembled the Pilgrim Fathers and Joshua Ben Nun.

Today, that discourse has fallen out of favor. So, while some right-wing Zionists still celebrate the ancient Israelites' religiously ordained invasion, today's dominant Jewish story—the one told by mainstream American Jewish organizations and by the Israeli government, particularly when speaking in English—replaces virtuous colonization with virtuous victimhood. No longer are Zionists equivalent to the Pilgrims who came ashore at Plymouth Rock. In a 2019 interview, the former Israeli ambassador to the United States Michael Oren compared Israeli Jews to the Sioux.

Jews today tend to avert our eyes from how we won the land and focus instead on how we lost it. The AJC pins the blame on the Roman Empire, which it claims expelled most Jews in 70 CE. In his 1993 book, *A Place Among the Nations,* Netanyahu adds an even more useful culprit: Arabs. Yes, Rome contributed to the "decline of Jewish power and presence in Palestine," he acknowledges. But the final blow came six hundred years later when a "steady stream of colonists" arrived from the Arabian Peninsula and "finally succeeded in doing what the might of Rome had not achieved: the uprooting of the Jewish farmer from his soil." In Netanyahu's telling, the Arabs become the Pilgrim Fathers. The Jews of antiquity were the Sioux, who "resisted conquest, occupation, and exile for nearly twenty centuries," until finally vanquished.

ONE MIGHT THINK that when it comes to Israel, we would cast this victimhood narrative aside. Zionism's core promise, after all, is to ensure that Jews are never powerless again. Israeli commentators often argue that refusing to be a victim is central to Israeli identity.

But while Israeli and diaspora Jews do not depict Israel as powerless, we do often portray it as persecuted—"the Jew of the nations," to use a popular establishment Jewish phrase—slandered, menaced, and delegitimized like no other country on earth. "The State of Israel, which its founders hoped would be fundamentally different from the diaspora," the historian Derek Penslar has noted, "is now seen as its extension—no less threatened, no less unjustly maligned."

This paradigm—Israel as the perpetual target of aggression, never its author—frames the Jewish establishment's rendition of Israeli history. Consider its account of the departure of more than half of the Arab population of British Mandatory Palestine during Israel's war of independence. "The Palestinian refugee issue originated in the 1948 Arab-Israeli war," explains the Anti-Defamation League (ADL), America's best-known organization fighting antisemitism, "when five Arab armies invaded the State of Israel just hours after it was established." The moral responsibility is clear: The Palestinians left their homes because Arab nations started a war. Palestinians suffered, but only because Israel was attacked.

The problem with this chronology is that between one-third and half of the Palestinians departed before May 14,

1948, when Israel declared independence and the Arab governments declared war. By the time the Arab armies attacked, Zionist forces had already largely depopulated Jaffa and Haifa, Palestine's two largest cities. The war's most notorious massacre of Palestinians, in which Zionist militias killed more than a hundred men, women, and children in the village of Deir Yassin, occurred in April. When Jewish leaders claim the Arab invasions drove Palestinians to leave, they've got the causality reversed. "It was not the entry of the Arab armies that caused the exodus. It was the exodus that caused the entry of the Arab armies," concluded the historian Walid Khalidi after consulting extensive Arab government documents and press reports.

For a Jewish establishment determined to depict Israel as "the Jew of the nations," forever blamed for sins it did not commit, these historical findings are inconvenient. But Israeli and American Jewish officials offer another argument for why the Arab governments, and not Israel, are to blame for roughly three-quarters of a million Palestinians leaving their homes: The Arab regimes told the Palestinians to leave. In *A Place Among the Nations*, Netanyahu argues that in many cases "Jews pleaded with their Palestinian Arab neighbors to stay. This was in sharp contrast to the directives the Palestinian Arabs were receiving from Arab governments, exhorting them to leave in order to clear the way for the invading armies."

This argument, too, is mostly fiction. A 1948 report by Israel's own intelligence service concluded that Zionist attacks accounted for roughly 70 percent of the Palestinian departures, while orders from Arab forces accounted for roughly

5 percent. Despite this, Jewish communal officials still often insist that Arabs, not Zionists, forced the Palestinians out. Nor do they grapple with one last, uncomfortable fact: Even if Palestinians did leave because Arab armies attacked, or because Arab governments urged them to, Israel still didn't let them return.

The harsh truth is that Zionist forces had to expel large numbers of Palestinians in order to create a Jewish-majority state. The prewar Palestinian population was simply too large. In November 1947, when the United Nations voted to partition Palestine into Jewish and Arab countries, Jews were only one-third of the population. Thus, even the state earmarked for Jews—which would have encompassed 55 percent of Mandatory Palestine—would have been almost half Palestinian. Since Jews lived largely in urban areas, Palestinians also owned 80 percent of the Jewish state's arable land. Zionist leaders knew that a country in which Palestinians were almost half the population and possessed most of the territory wouldn't constitute a genuine Jewish state. Jews would not rule. A month after the UN vote, Ben-Gurion told members of his political party, "Only a state with at least 80 percent Jews is a viable and stable state." So, while Ben-Gurion and the Zionist leadership—unlike their Palestinian and Arab counterparts—accepted the UN partition plan, they also began expelling Palestinians because that was the only way to create a large Jewish majority that occupied most of the land.

On this point, Benny Morris, the Israeli historian who gained fame for his research into the Palestinian exodus, has been unusually frank. "Ben-Gurion was a transferist," Morris told the Israeli journalist Ari Shavit in a 2004 interview. "He understood that there could be no Jewish state with a large and hostile Arab minority in its midst." Perhaps taken aback by Morris's directness, Shavit observed, "I don't hear you condemning him." Indeed, Morris was not. "Ben-Gurion was right," Morris continued. "If he had not done what he did, a state would not have come into being. That has to be clear. It is impossible to evade."

But it is possible to evade. Among the Jewish state's high-profile, English-language defenders, Morris is an outlier, a throwback to the early Zionists who bluntly defended Zionist conquest. That's why you won't find him on the ADL or AIPAC lecture circuit. Their narrative is built on evasion because they know it's not possible, in a postcolonial age, to acknowledge the truth about why Palestinians became refugees without raising questions about why they and their descendants can't return. George Orwell famously wrote that since forthrightly defending Stalin's purges or British colonialism in India required "arguments which are too brutal for most people to face," their public justification "has to consist largely of euphemism, question-begging and sheer cloudy vagueness." That perfectly captures establishment Jewish discourse about 1948. The only way to depict Israel as the victim of its own mass expulsion of Palestinians is to evade what Palestinians actually endured. Euphemism is the point.

Consider what the Palestinian expulsion looks like when recounted without euphemism. Amid the crush of people fleeing Haifa as Zionist forces attacked, a woman named Nazmiyya al-Kilani walked with a broken leg, one child in her arms and another tied to her apron so he wouldn't be swallowed up by the crowd, to the city's port, where she boarded a boat to Acre, which was itself depopulated after Zionist forces shut off the city's electricity and water. In the chaos, she lost contact with her husband, father, brother, and sisters, all of whom were deported to Syria. She didn't see them for another fifty years.

That fall, Israeli troops entered the largely Catholic and Greek Orthodox Palestinian village of Eilaboun in the Galilee. According to the filmmaker Hisham Zreiq, who used oral histories, Israeli documents, and a UN observer report to reconstruct events, the troops were met by priests holding a white flag. Soldiers from the Golani Brigade responded by assembling villagers in the town square. They forced the bulk of Eilaboun's residents to evacuate the village and head north, thus serving as human shields for Israeli forces who trailed behind them, in case the road was mined. After forcing the villagers to walk all day with little food or water, the soldiers robbed them of their valuables and loaded them on trucks that deposited them across the Lebanese border. According to an eyewitness, the roughly dozen men held back in the town square were executed in groups of three.

The people of Eilaboun were comparatively lucky: some were allowed to return. During Israel's war of independence, Zionist forces depopulated roughly four hundred Palestinian villages. Many were looted. Most were totally destroyed.

Listen to every one of Benjamin Netanyahu's speeches about Israel's creation, and the speeches of every establishment American Jewish leader, and you won't hear a single story like Nazmiyya al-Kilani's. You will not learn the name, or be invited to imagine the experience, of a single Palestinian whom Zionist forces expelled. That is not an accident. Only by erasing the names and experiences of ordinary Palestinians can they be made authors of their own expulsion. We evade the harsh realities of 1948 just as we evade the end of the book of Esther. In this way, Israel's creation is made to fit the script.

THIS ISN'T ONLY the story we tell ourselves about Israel's past. It's also our story about Israel's present. The plot goes like this. We have finally achieved what every other people takes for granted: a state of our own. Yet in the case of Jews, and Jews alone, that right is contested. So even with a state, we remain victims.

Our communal leaders call this right self-determination. "Denying the Jewish people the same right to self-determination that you would extend to other people," ADL CEO Jonathan Greenblatt asserted in 2020, constitutes one of the "modern manifestations of the oldest hatred, anti-Semitism." But self-determination means determination of the self, not others. Just as one person cannot invoke their individual right to self-determination to control another person, one group of people cannot invoke their collective right to control another group. As the Israeli philosophers Avishai Margalit and Joseph Raz have explained, "Those who may benefit from self-government cannot insist on it at all costs. Their interests have to be considered along those of others."

That's why the world was unimpressed by the South African defense minister P. W. Botha's claim, in 1977, to be defending "the right of self-determination of the white nation." Because he wasn't defending self-determination. He was defending supremacy. When Jewish leaders say self-determination is a universal right, they're employing the same sleight of hand. Self-determination may be a universal right if it means communal autonomy. Few would quibble with a school in a largely Afrikaner town teaching children in Afrikaans, so long as white and Black South Africans live under the same law. But there is no universal right to a state in which your tribe rules everyone else.

Yet, in Israel, that's what Jews do. Israel controls all the territory between the Jordan River and the Mediterranean Sea. That includes the West Bank, where, although Israel has since 1993 subcontracted certain functions to the Palestinian Authority, Israeli soldiers—and the soldiers of no other army—can enter any square inch of territory anytime they want and arrest anyone they want, including the Palestinian Authority's own officials. Israel also controls the Gaza Strip, even though it withdrew its soldiers and settlers in 2005 (before reinvading after October 7). Israel controls Gaza because it controls all access to the Strip by air and sea as well as two of the three land crossings. (Even at the third, Rafah, which borders Egypt, Israel wields substantial authority over who and what can legally pass.) As the Israeli human rights group Gisha has noted, Israel even controls what type of vegetables Palestinians in Gaza can legally export. Before the current war, Israel tried to control Gaza in the way guards would control a prison if they left the interior and arrayed themselves along the perimeter, thus determining—at gunpoint—what is allowed in and out.

Inside all this territory that Israel controls live more than seven million Palestinians. Roughly 70 percent of them—the residents of the West Bank and Gaza—aren't even citizens of the state that dominates their lives. The other 30 percent, sometimes called Arab Israelis, do enjoy citizenship, but of a profoundly second-class kind. They can vote and serve in parliament but attend segregated schools and cannot marry Jews inside Israel since Israel has no civil marriage. Israel also severely disadvantages Palestinian citizens in its allocation of land. More than 90 percent of the territory in Israel proper is managed by the Israel Land Authority, which allocates almost half the seats on its governing body to the Jewish National Fund, an entity that has stated bluntly that it "does not have an allegiance to the Israeli public. Its allegiance is to the Jewish people." It's as if most of America's land were overseen by an institution largely controlled by Christians who want it developed solely for Christian use. This helps explain why the cities and towns in which most Palestinian citizens live are so overcrowded. According to a 2013 report by the Israel Democracy Institute, the average Palestinian-majority municipality encompasses roughly one-sixth as much land per person as its Jewish counterpart.

Attend a forum on Israel at most American synagogues or listen to an Israeli official being interviewed on TV, and you're unlikely to hear about Israeli land law or the separate legal systems that govern Jewish citizens and Palestinian noncitizens in the West Bank, or the rules that determine when Palestinians can leave the Gaza Strip. That's no accident. It's because any genuine inquiry into Palestinian life under Israeli control would expose the duplicity of claiming that Israel offers Jews mere "self-determination." When a Jewish state denies most of its Palestinian residents citizenship and denies all of them legal equality, it is not merely offering Jews the right to determine their own lives. It is offering them dominance over another people. And under international law, there is a word for legal dominance based on ethnicity, religion, or race—a word that Human Rights Watch, Amnesty International, and even Israel's own leading human rights group, B'Tselem, say applies to Israel. It is not "self-determination." It is "apartheid."

Apartheid is violent. Because Palestinians in Gaza live under the control of a state that is not accountable to them—whose citizenship they cannot attain and whose leaders they cannot choose—most have spent the bulk of their lives under blockade, unable to leave a territory less than half the size of New York City that Human Rights Watch calls an "open-air prison." Because Palestinians in the West Bank live under the control of a state that is not accountable to them, Israeli authorities routinely jail their children. Between 2000 and 2023, Israel detained more than 13,000 Palestinian children, according to estimates by Defense for Children International-Palestine (DCIP). Of the 766 West Bank children that DCIP interviewed, it found that 97 percent had been interrogated without a family member present, 75 percent had suffered physical violence, and 23 percent had been held for at least two days in solitary confinement.

Nor are Israel's Palestinian citizens spared the violence that accompanies inferiority under the law. Confined to overcrowded enclaves by decades of land expropriation and discriminatory planning policies, they have little choice but to build illegally. Which means their homes are often bulldozed.

In 2018, the last year for which data is available, Palestinian Israelis received more than 88 percent of the demolition orders issued within Israel proper. This figure doesn't even include many Bedouins in the Negev desert, whom the state considers illegal "squatters" on their own land. In 2018, Israel demolished more than seventeen times as many Bedouin buildings as it demolished in the entire rest of the country (excluding the West Bank and East Jerusalem). Since 2010, the Bedouin village of Al-Araqib has been demolished more than two hundred times.

Mainstream Jewish discourse rarely acknowledges the violence inherent in legalized inequality. It does the opposite: it characterizes as violent, even genocidal, the prospect of equality under the law. In 2018, three Palestinian members of Israel's Knesset proposed a "basic law"—one that carries constitutional-level weight—to enshrine "the principle of equal citizenship for every citizen" and prohibit "discrimination on grounds of nationality, race, religion, gender, language, color, political outlook, ethnic origin or social status." Israel's Knesset speaker, who hails from Netanyahu's Likud Party, would not even allow it to be debated because it would "gnaw at the foundations of the state." Like those Palestinian parliamentarians, the national anti-Zionist organizations with the greatest influence on American campuses explicitly call for equality. Yet Netanyahu says they desire Israel's "annihilation." The word choice—"annihilation"—is not accidental. It is designed to associate Palestinian equality with Jewish death.

That's also the implication of the phrase "right to exist." It implies that if Jewish supremacy doesn't exist, Israel's Jews won't either. Jewish officials use "right to exist"—like "self-determination"—to suggest that the world denies Israel the legitimacy it grants all other countries. "Israel is the only UN member state whose very right to exist is under constant challenge," declared David Harris, then the CEO of the American Jewish Committee, in 2020. In 2022, the World Jewish Congress claimed that "no other country's existence is called into question" except Israel's. But the phrase "right to exist" conflates two very different things: a state and its political system. Max Weber famously defined a state as the entity in a given territory that possesses a "monopoly of legitimate physical violence." Except for a few anarchists, no one questions whether a state—or perhaps two—should exist between the Jordan River and the Mediterranean Sea. What they question is a political system that the world's leading human rights groups say constitutes apartheid. That doesn't single Israel out. Americans challenge the legitimacy of foreign political systems all the time. While student activists question Jewish supremacy in Israel, members of Congress question whether communist parties should run China, Cuba, and North Korea, whether a military junta should run Myanmar, whether tyrannical clerics should run Iran, whether a personalized dictatorship should run Russia, and whether a homicidal prince should run Saudi Arabia. Often, they punish the political systems they don't like by imposing sanctions—the very action campus protesters propose taking against Israel.

One reason people confuse Israel as a state and Jewish supremacy as a political system is that Israel's name itself connotes Jewish supremacy. "Israel" isn't only the name of a country. It's also the name of the Jewish people, and thus suggests a political system built for Jews, not for everyone living in the land. That's certainly how most Israeli Jews see it. In a 2019 poll by the Jewish People Policy Institute, 75 percent of them agreed with the statement "To be a real Israeli, you must be Jewish."

In this regard, Israel is unlike South Africa, whose name has no ethnic, religious, or racial connotations, and thus remained after apartheid fell. It is more like the People's Republic of China, which indicates Communist Party control, or the Islamic Republic of Iran, which indicates clerical rule. Were Israel to become a state based on legal equality, as those Palestinian Knesset members proposed, its name might become "Israel-Palestine" or "Palestine-Israel" or perhaps something else that does not connote group supremacy. But this change would hardly be unprecedented. When Rhodesia—named for the British imperialist Cecil Rhodes— abandoned white rule, it changed its name to Zimbabwe. When Albania, Angola, Benin, Bulgaria, Mongolia, and many other countries abandoned their communist political systems in the early 1990s, they lopped off "People's Republic" from their official names. If critics imagine renaming Israel because its name implies a supremacist political system, that isn't unique. Israel isn't being singled out. It's not being made a victim.

None of this is to say that Jews can't be victims. Of course we can. Jews have been victims of some of the worst atrocities in history. That history remains deep within many of us. I have walked through the district in northern Lithuania where my paternal grandmother was born, and through the forests where its Jews were murdered. I have led Shabbat services in Rhodes, in a sixteenth-century synagogue that gathers a minyan only when the remnants of that shattered community return from distant corners of the globe. Many Jews have experiences like this. The problem with our communal story is not that it acknowledges the crimes we have suffered. The problem is that it ignores the crimes we commit. We are forever Esther and our detractors are forever Haman, even when a nuclear-armed Jewish state subjugates millions of Palestinians who lack citizenship in the country they've inhabited for their entire lives. By seeing a Jewish state as forever abused, never the abuser, we deny its capacity for evil. Before October 7, I thought I understood the dangers of this way of thinking. Turns out I had no idea.

2

To Whom Evil Is Done

L ife in the Jewish communities near Gaza was difficult even before October 7. Lilya Ann—she has not publicly disclosed her last name—is a slender twenty-six-year-old with straight brown hair and tattoos across her arms and collarbone. She grew up in Sderot, less than a mile from the Gaza border, hearing sirens. She could not always make it to a shelter in the ten seconds before rockets hit. Several landed close to her. At age four, she began experiencing panic attacks.

On October 7, Hamas fighters downed one of Sderot's electricity poles. At home with her family, with the doors locked and blinds drawn, Lilya Ann spent the night in total darkness. As explosions boomed outside, she suffered the worst panic attack of her life. Fortunately, the fighters never entered her house, and she escaped Sderot the next morning.

She was among the lucky ones. On the morning of October 7, Liza Idan called her daughter-in-law, Smadar, in Kibbutz Kfar Aza, located three miles from Gaza. Her six-year-old granddaughter, Amalia, answered the phone and said that her parents and younger sister, Avigail, were dead. Liza asked if she'd been watching a scary movie. Amalia repeated, "Mom, Dad, and Avigail are dead," and hung up the phone.

Earlier that morning, a Hamas fighter had entered Amalia's home and murdered her mother. Another militant soon killed her father. Amalia and her older brother, Michael, aged nine, hid in a dark closet, without food or water, for fourteen hours. When Israeli soldiers finally arrived, the children were initially too terrified to open the door or even speak. They later learned that their three-year-old sister, Avigail, was still alive. Covered in her father's blood, she had run to a neighbor's house and been taken hostage. Seven weeks later, after turning four in captivity, she was released.

For some Israelis, captivity lasted far longer than that. David Cunio, an electrician from Kibbutz Nir Oz, located one and a half miles from Gaza, was at home on October 7 with his wife, Sharon, and their twin three-year-old daughters, Emma and Yuli. Early that morning, they were ordered into their safe room and told to keep the doors shut. Five hours later, Hamas fighters entered the house. They could not force their way into the safe room. So, they lit the house on fire.

As smoke rose, David climbed out of the window with Yuli and was captured. Sharon lost consciousness, but the fighters dragged her out. David, Sharon, and Yuli were then taken to Gaza. At first, they were kept in a private home, then taken to a hospital, where they eventually reunited with their other daughter, Emma, who had also been taken hostage and had been held alone in Gaza—with no bathing and minimal food—for roughly ten days. In a small room on the hospital's first floor, the Cunios lived with twelve other hostages, without regular access to a bathroom. Food was scarce, often moldy pita and small amounts of cheese. In less than two months, Sharon lost twenty-four pounds.

On the day Sharon learned that she and her daughters would be released but that her husband would not, the couple held each other for three hours. David was later taken into a tunnel underneath Gaza.

There are more than a thousand stories like these. They would devastate any nation. But they had a special impact on Israelis, many of whom already harbored traumatic memories of violence. Tel Aviv University's National Center for Traumatic Stress and Resilience reported that after the attack Israeli military veterans began experiencing long-dormant symptoms of PTSD. The massacre transported Mona Yahia back to 1969, when her family hid in their home while their Baghdad neighbors cheered the hanging of nine Iraqi Jews accused of being spies. At the age of eighty-three, Zili Wenkert, who had survived the Transnistria concentration camp, watched a video of her twenty-two-year-old grandson, Omer, handcuffed and stripped to his underwear, inside an SUV headed for Gaza. "My grandson in the hands of Hamas—it is something I cannot process," she told a reporter. "This is my real Holocaust."

There is no comparing October 7's effect on Jewish Israelis—many of whom spent the days after the attack attending funerals, relocating after being forced from their homes, and being called into military service—with its impact on Jews thousands of miles away. But even in its radically attenuated form, the massacre had a seismic effect. October 7 was not only Shabbat. In the United States, it was also the holiday of Shemini Atzeret, which is followed by Simchat Torah, the end of the annual cycle of Torah reading and normally one of the most joyous days of the year. On these holidays, observant Jews refrain from using electronic devices. In my community, that meant many people could not access direct information about the attack for almost two days after it happened. I will never forget trying to dance, as is customary on Simchat Torah, while knowing that something horrifying had just happened, but not knowing exactly what. And I will never forget how members of our synagogue asked non-Jews to turn on their phones—since they were not permitted to do so themselves—in order to find out whether their friends and family in Israel were still alive.

After the holiday, when I learned that roughly 250 Israelis had been taken captive, I thought of Gilad Shalit. When Hamas held him captive between 2006 and 2011, you could hardly enter an American Jewish institution without seeing his face. After October 7, many American Jews tried to do something similar—to visualize the hostages so they would be neither forgotten nor treated as mere statistics. Our family printed out their names and put them on our refrigerator door. But there were too many names to remember, too many faces to envision. The scale was overwhelming.

Something else was different too. I don't recall seeing an image of Gilad Shalit defaced or torn down. This time, however, it happened regularly. For months, I couldn't walk down the street without seeing disfigured hostage posters. Maybe the vandals saw themselves as merely protesting Israel's devastating assault on Gaza. But they were also erasing, or mocking, Israeli suffering. And it wasn't just them. A letter from

Israeli progressives to leftists in the United States and Europe noted that "individuals who were, until now, our political partners, have reacted with indifference to" Hamas's attack and "sometimes even justified Hamas's actions." In those early days I scoured antiwar essays and speeches for expressions of outrage at the murder of hundreds of Israeli civilians. Often, they weren't there. As the weeks passed, I again and again heard the slogan "Resistance is justified when people are occupied," as if October 7 had not just happened, as if Hamas—a corrupt and despotic organization with a long history of brutality against both Israelis and Palestinians—had not just murdered and tortured more than a thousand souls. As if there were no moral distinction between boycotting a product, initiating a protest, shooting a soldier, and killing a child.

When I felt most estranged, I imagined my grandmother asking why I was surprised. Some people want to kill Jews, I heard her say. Many others don't mind. It's nothing new. This is how it is.

IN THE DAYS after October 7, that message was everywhere. Five days after the attack, ten American Jewish organizations labeled October 7 a "modern-day pogrom." On October 17, Netanyahu called Hamas "the new Nazis." On October 28, he compared the group to Amalek, Haman's biblical ancestors, whose memory the book of Deuteronomy commands the Israelites to "blot out." On October 30, Israel's ambassador to the United Nations, Gilad Erdan, told the UN Security Council that on October 7 "entire Israeli families were turned into smoke and ash—no different than the fate my grandfather's family met in Auschwitz." Near the end of his speech, he rose from his seat and affixed a yellow star to his jacket.

Some Israeli officials restricted these analogies to Hamas. Others applied them to Palestinians writ large. On October 16, Boaz Bismuth, a Knesset member from Netanyahu's Likud Party, asserted that "the cruel and monstrous 'innocent civilians' from Gaza also took an active part in the pogrom inside the Israeli settlements. . . . We must not show mercy to cruel people, there is no room for any humanitarian gesture—the memory of Amalek must be wiped out." On November 27, commenting on a poll that showed widespread Palestinian support for the attack, the Israeli finance minister, Bezalel Smotrich, declared that "there are 2 million Nazis" in the West Bank.

I know where these comparisons come from. In moments of bewilderment and pain, people search their storehouse of collective memory to make sense of the trauma. After the massacre, our synagogue began weekly recitations of a prayer that recalls "the pious, the upright, the pure, the holy congregations which laid down their lives in sanctification of God." It was written roughly a thousand years ago, when crusaders slaughtered Jewish communities along the Rhine.

But while these historical analogies anchor us, they also cloud our vision. They keep us from recognizing that, in crucial ways, Palestinian violence is unlike the violence perpetrated against Jews in the past. The Jews who suffered pogroms in the Russian Empire in the late nineteenth and early twentieth centuries, and the Jews who faced genocide in Europe in the 1940s, were members of a vulnerable minority living in countries that had long restricted their rights. The terror they experienced was inextricably bound up with the oppression they endured. In Israel, by contrast, Jews enjoy legal supremacy, and it is Palestinians who lack basic freedoms. Comparing October 7 to the Holocaust or a pogrom ignores that fundamental difference. To preserve Israel's innocence, it transforms Palestinians from a subjugated people into the reincarnation of the monsters of the Jewish past, the latest manifestation of the eternal, pathological, genocidal hatred that, according to the Passover Haggadah, "in every generation rises up to destroy us."

There are better analogies. October 7 has more in common with the murder, torture, and rape of thousands of Europeans in newly independent Haiti in 1804, or the Fort Mims massacre of white settlers by Creek Indians in what is now Alabama in 1813, or the Lari massacre by Mau Mau rebels seeking to overthrow British colonialism in Kenya in 1953—gruesome, pitiless attacks by oppressed peoples resisting dispossession. For many Jews today, pondering these analogies is alien and uncomfortable—the equivalent of imagining Hagar murdering Abraham and Sarah or the seven nations of Canaan massacring the forces of Joshua Ben Nun. They alter the script that explains who we are.

But earlier generations of Zionists, who were less invested in Jewish innocence, made such comparisons themselves. "Every native population in the world resists colonists as long as it has the slightest hope of being able to rid itself of the danger of being colonized," wrote Jabotinsky in 1923. "That is what the Arabs in Palestine are doing." Six years later, after Palestinians killed 133 Jews in Hebron, Safed, and elsewhere, Hans Kohn, a Zionist official in Jerusalem who would later become a renowned scholar of nationalism, called the violence inevitable. "Of course, the Arabs attacked us in August," he wrote. "Since they have no armies, they could not obey the rules of war. They perpetrated all the barbaric acts that are characteristic of a colonial revolt. But we are obliged to look into the deeper cause of this revolt," which he attributed to the refusal of Zionists to seek "the consent of the indigenous people" for their effort to settle Mandatory Palestine. In 1956, when Palestinians ambushed and killed a young security officer in a kibbutz near the Gaza Strip, the Israeli chief of staff, Moshe Dayan, delivered a stunningly frank obituary. "Let us not cast the blame on the murderers today," he declared. "For eight years they have been sitting in the refugee camps in Gaza, and before their eyes we have been transforming the lands and the villages, where they and their fathers dwelt, into our estate." Writing about Palestinian armed resistance in 1976, the Israeli social critic Yeshayahu Leibowitz declared, "In our times of worldwide decolonization, a colonial regime necessarily gives birth to terrorism."

These writers were not condoning Palestinian violence. They were seeking to understand it. The responses they favored differed. Jabotinsky and Dayan wanted to crush Palestinian resistance. Kohn turned against a Jewish state. Leibowitz urged Israel to return the West Bank and Gaza Strip. But none saw Palestinians as Nazis, pogromists, or Amalek. They understood that violent dispossession and violent resistance are intertwined.

It's hard to talk so frankly today. In many Jewish communities, even many Jewish families, suggesting that October 7 stems from anything but Hamas's pure evil is a ticket to excommunication. Soon after the massacre, one of our closest family friends asked my wife whether we believed that Israel bore any responsibility for the carnage. She answered yes. He said he would never speak to us again.

Earlier in my life, I might have shared his fury. What changed my perspective on Palestinian violence—and led me away from the analogies with Nazis and pogroms—was encountering Israeli violence. In my early thirties, when I first visited Palestinians in the West Bank, a woman told me that when she gave birth to a boy, one of her daughters started to cry. The woman explained that the Israeli army often entered homes in their village looking to arrest boys who had thrown stones and that if you had a son, it meant your home would likely be invaded, whether he was a stone thrower or not. That's why her daughter cried when her brother was born. On a later trip I walked through an entire village slated for demolition. To encourage its residents to leave, the Israeli army had already disabled the local well. The people I met, whose only crime was being Palestinian in a part of the West Bank where Israel doesn't want Palestinians to live, woke up every day wondering when the bulldozers would come.

IN THE YEARS that followed, as my children grew older, I sometimes imagined how they and the other teenagers at their Jewish school might react if a foreign army humiliated their parents, invaded their homes, or took their land. And I came to understand what Jabotinsky, Kohn, Dayan, and Leibowitz were trying to say.

Israeli oppression isn't the only cause of Palestinian violence. Palestinians, like all people, are responsible for their actions. But Israeli oppression makes Palestinian violence far more likely. Among academics, the point isn't controversial. In a 2004 study of Palestinian suicide bombers during the second intifada, the economist Basel Saleh found that almost half had suffered at the hands of the Israeli military: either they had been arrested or injured, or they had seen a family member injured, arrested, or killed. "Personal grievances," he concluded, "have a considerable weight in motivating attacks." A 2006 paper by two University of Toronto sociologists reached a similar conclusion. Most Palestinian suicide bombers "gave up their lives to avenge the killing of a close relative, as retribution for specific attacks against the Palestinian people or as payback for perceived attacks against Islam." A 2014 study by Israeli political scientists determined that among both Palestinians and Israelis "individual-level exposure to terrorism and political violence makes the subject populations less likely to support peace efforts."

The life stories of Hamas's and Islamic Jihad's leaders illustrate the point. In November 1956, the Israeli military entered Gaza, then under Egyptian control, after Cairo blockaded the Straits of Tiran. In the town of Khan Younis, according to Benny Morris, "IDF troops shot dead hundreds of Palestinian refugees and local inhabitants in the town" while searching for weapons. A nine-year-old boy named Abdel el-Aziz al-Rantisi saw his uncle shot. "I still remember the wailing and tears of my father over his brother," al-Rantisi told an interviewer many years later. "I couldn't sleep for many months after that. . . . [T]hey planted hatred in our hearts." Three-year-old Ziad al-Nakhalah witnessed the execution of his father. Three decades later, al-Rantisi helped found Hamas. Al-Nakhalah now leads its smaller but equally militant rival, Palestinian Islamic Jihad. Over the decades, this pattern has repeated itself over and over. Gershon Baskin, an Israeli hostage negotiator who has spent countless hours with Hamas leaders, notes that "they recruit Hamas fighters from early ages from bereaved families immediately after each round of conflict."

If Palestinians were Nazis, Palestinian public opinion about killing Israelis would remain fairly steady. Instead, notes the pollster Khalil Shikaki, Palestinian support "for violence is not stable; it responds to threat perception, to the level of pain and suffering imposed by the policies and actions of Israel."

Chart Palestinian politics over the last three decades and you can see Shikaki's point. Palestinian support for violence goes up when Palestinian hopes of freedom go down.

In the 1993 Oslo Accords, named for the Norwegian city where negotiations began, Yasser Arafat's Palestine Liberation Organization (PLO) recognized Israel and renounced armed resistance. These were historic concessions. The PLO publicly abandoned both the goal it had been seeking since its founding—a Palestinian state from the Jordan River to the Mediterranean Sea—and the principal method it had been using to pursue it. Yet polls showed widespread Palestinian support because Palestinians believed that the newly created Palestinian Authority, which gave them a measure of self-government in the West Bank and Gaza, would soon become their own sovereign state.

Hamas denounced the PLO's concessions and tried to

sabotage the talks. In April 1993, it launched the first of what would be many suicide bombings. But Palestinians over-whelmingly disapproved of these attacks. In the fall of 1995, according to Shikaki's polling, only 18 percent of Palestinians supported violence against Israelis.

That changed after Benjamin Netanyahu became prime minister in 1996. Hamas's violence undermined Israelis' hopes that the negotiations would bring security. They responded by electing a candidate who had opposed Oslo from its inception and would later boast that his refusal to cede significant territory to the Palestinians "stopped the Oslo Accord." Netanyahu also accelerated settlement growth in the West Bank, where Palestinians hoped to build their state. The number of new settler housing units more than doubled, from under two thousand in 1996, to more than forty-three hundred in 1998, Netanyahu's last full year in office. While Palestinians had expected the Palestinian Authority to encompass most of the West Bank, by the late 1990s it still governed only an archipelago of disconnected villages and towns while Israel controlled all the territory in between. When Israel closed off that territory to Palestinian travel, as it did frequently—in response to security fears or even during Jewish holidays—it paralyzed Palestinian life. The results were predictable: Palestinians' faith that they would achieve a state plummeted, and by January 1999, near the end of Netanyahu's time as prime minister, support for armed attacks had risen to more than 50 percent.

Netanyahu lost that year to the more moderate Ehud Barak, and Palestinian support for violence briefly dipped.

But although new settlement construction initially declined, it rose in 2000—Barak's first full year in office—to an even higher level than under Netanyahu. Barak also reneged on a scheduled Israeli withdrawal from parts of the West Bank.

When Barak and Arafat met at Camp David in the summer of 2000, the Israeli prime minster made an offer that most Jewish Israelis considered generous, even reckless. But to most Palestinians, it fell far short of the state they hoped Oslo would deliver. It let Israel annex an array of West Bank settlements while also retaining control of the Jordan valley, which forms the West Bank's border with Jordan, for at least a decade. Altogether, roughly 20 percent of the West Bank would have remained in Israel's hands, and a thin wedge of Israeli-annexed territory, running west to east, would have bisected the new Palestinian state. Israel would have also controlled Palestine's airspace, electromagnetic spectrum, and most of its water resources. Palestinians would have gained a capital in outlying areas of Arab East Jerusalem but not its urban core, and they would not have enjoyed sovereignty over Jerusalem's Temple Mount, which contains the Al-Aqsa Mosque, the third-holiest site in Islam. Barak would allow a token number of Palestinian refugees to go back to Israel proper but would not acknowledge Israel's role in their expulsion nor concede that refugees had a right to return.

For many Palestinians, who believed that having conceded 78 percent of Mandatory Palestine to Israel, they should govern a sovereign country encompassing the entirety of the rest, this was woefully inadequate. The Palestinian leadership reportedly proposed allowing Israel to annex settlements on only 2.5 percent of the West Bank and demanded a rapid transition to Palestinian control of the Jordan valley—which Barak refused.

This disillusionment laid the foundation for the violence that followed. After the talks failed, the right-wing Israeli leader Ariel Sharon visited the ultrasensitive Temple Mount surrounded by a thousand Israeli police. Palestinians began throwing stones, and Israeli forces responded harshly, firing roughly one million bullets and killing fifty people in the first three weeks of the revolt. Palestinians escalated to suicide bombings, and the bloody second intifada began.

In the spring of 2000, when the former Senate majority leader George Mitchell published an investigation into the violence that followed Sharon's visit, he criticized Arafat for not doing more to contain the initial disturbances and Israel for cracking down on them so harshly. But these were merely triggers. The deeper cause was despair. Palestinians no longer believed that Oslo would bring them freedom. According to Shikaki, "The loss of confidence in the ability of the peace process to deliver a permanent agreement on acceptable terms had a dramatic impact on the level of Palestinian support for violence against Israelis." Marwan Barghouti, a Palestinian leader who had supported Oslo but was arrested during the second intifada for helping to plan attacks that killed Israeli civilians, told an Israeli journalist that he had "reached a simple conclusion. You don't want to end the occupation and you don't want to stop the settlements, so the only way to convince you is by force."

In late December, President Bill Clinton tried to save the day. He outlined parameters for a final deal that split the difference between the Israeli and the Palestinian positions. Both sides said yes to Clinton's terms and then expressed reservations that transformed yes into maybe. Negotiations continued into the new year, but Israel's government was collapsing. Weeks away from an election it seemed certain to lose, Barak's coalition retained the support of barely more than one-third of Israel's parliament. Even if Israeli and Palestinian negotiators had been able to agree, the moment of opportunity had passed. The talks ended, Sharon became Israel's new prime minister, and the second intifada raged on for four more years.

Finally, in 2005, after more than one thousand Israelis and over three thousand Palestinians had been killed, the second intifada ended. As the fighting was subsiding, Arafat died and Mahmoud Abbas—favored in Washington for his opposition to armed resistance—replaced him as head of the Palestinian Authority, which still governed Palestinians in the West Bank and Gaza, although Israel retained ultimate control. Abbas soon faced a challenge. In 2006, after Israel withdrew its settlements from the Gaza Strip, Palestinians held parliamentary elections in the West Bank, Gaza, and East Jerusalem, which Hamas won. But under pressure from the United States, Abbas repudiated the results and disbanded parliament. When his forces tried to push Hamas out of Gaza, its political stronghold, the effort backfired. Hamas violently wrested control of the Strip in fratricidal fighting that took 161 Palestinian lives. Israel, which already controlled most access in and out of Gaza, responded by imposing a blockade.

What followed was a natural experiment on the efficacy

of renouncing armed resistance. In 2007, Abbas appointed a prime minister, Salam Fayyad, whose antipathy to Palestinian violence and efforts to fight corruption drew applause in both Washington and Jerusalem. Meanwhile, in Gaza, Hamas stockpiled weapons, dug tunnels, and lobbed rockets. Six years later, Fayyad stepped down from his position and declared defeat. "In deeds, Israel never got behind me," he told the *New York Times* columnist Roger Cohen. "In fact, it was quite hostile. The occupation regime is more entrenched, with no sign it is beginning to relinquish its grip on our life." His failure, he predicted, would leave Hamas "strengthened."

While Abbas and Fayyad were collaborating with Israel, other Palestinians pursued a different alternative to Hamas: nonviolent protest. In 2005, Palestinian civil society organizations launched the Boycott, Divestment, and Sanctions movement, which was modeled on the movement to boycott apartheid South Africa. Israel made endorsing such boycotts a crime, and establishment American Jewish groups promoted legislation punishing Americans who participated in them. Palestinians appealed to the United Nations, but the United States repeatedly scuttled resolutions criticizing Israeli behavior at the Security Council. Palestinians also urged investigations of Israeli behavior by the International Criminal Court (ICC), which both Democratic and Republican presidents worked to quash.

Finally, in the spring of 2018, Palestinians in Gaza launched the Great March of Return, in which Palestinians marched toward the fence separating Gaza from Israel. Hamas did not initiate the demonstrations; marchers carried Palestinian, not Hamas, flags. But Hamas embraced the movement once the protests gained widespread support—even pausing its rocket fire. As demonstrators approached the fence, Israeli snipers shot them, generally below the knee, often maiming them for life. That spring, Gaza established an amputee soccer club. The Palestinian Centre for Human Rights and the Israeli human rights group B'Tselem reported that "over the course of the protests, Israeli security forces killed 223 Palestinians and injured more than 8,000. The vast majority of casualties were unarmed and posed no threat to anyone."

Consider the message Israel sent to Palestinians by responding that way to a largely unarmed march. I'm often told that if Palestinians weren't so murderous, rejectionist, incompetent, and pigheaded, they'd have their own country by now. And it's true that Palestinian leaders have not only made mistakes but also committed crimes. Hamas's suicide bombings, which helped elect Netanyahu, were a strategic and moral disaster. So was the second intifada. Mahmoud Abbas is a corrupt authoritarian who dabbles in revisionist theories of the Holocaust.

But here's the problem with our community's tendency to blame Palestinians for their own oppression. Even when Palestinians do the very things Jews ask of them—when they recognize Israel, help the Israeli military keep Israelis safe, and protest nonviolently—Jewish institutions still act the same way. Israel didn't stop bulldozing Palestinian homes when the PLO recognized its existence. AIPAC didn't demand a settlement freeze when Fayyad became prime minister. The ADL didn't start condemning the imprisonment of Palestinian children when Palestinians employed nonviolence. We demand that Palestinians produce Gandhis, and when they do, American Jewish organizations work to criminalize their boycotts and Israeli soldiers shoot them in the knees. No matter what strategy Palestinians employ in their fight for freedom, the Israeli government and its American Jewish allies work to ensure that it fails.

That work has been highly effective. By 2023, a wide array of Palestinian tactics—including security cooperation, calls to boycott, appeals to international institutions, and protest marches—had all been largely defeated. On the ground, conditions kept deteriorating. The settler population in the West Bank and East Jerusalem had close to tripled since Oslo began. The UN reported that settler attacks that year reached their highest rate since the institution began collecting data in 2006.

For West Bank Palestinians, life was not only precarious. It was often Kafkaesque. Consider the example of a Palestinian American truck driver named Kayed Abu Awwad. In the summer of 2023, he sold his house in Oak Lawn, Illinois, and prepared to move to the house his father had built in the West Bank town of Turmus Ayya. He wanted his American kids to learn "the language and culture" of their homeland. He knew that living in the West Bank came with risks. That January, settlers had shattered eight of his house's windows and sprayed it with graffiti. But Kayed paid for the windows to be repaired and shipped his furniture from the United States. Then, in June, settlers returned and torched the front part of the house. When Kayed and his family arrived two weeks later, they were forced to live with neighbors, crowded into a single room. As he began rebuilding the house yet again, he considered erecting a fence for additional protection but was told that Israeli authorities would never grant him a permit. If built without one, the fence could be demolished, and he might face a hefty fine.

Conditions in Gaza were worse. The Strip was "unlivable," according to the United Nations, largely because of its lack of electricity and clean water. The ocean off its coast had grown putrid since Gaza's sewage plants, lacking sufficient electricity to treat wastewater, pumped it into the sea. In the second quarter of 2023, youth unemployment was roughly 60 percent. Among recent university graduates, it was 70 percent. The journalist Muhammad Shehada, who grew up in Gaza, told me that his friends there sometimes quipped that they could not even afford to fall in love since they lacked the money to leave their parents' homes. Once in their twenties, many stopped wishing each other happy birthday since every passing year was a painful reminder of their inability to build independent lives. In 2020, Shehada wrote an essay about suicide. In Islam, he explained, "suicide is an unforgivable sin that leads to eternity in hell." Nonetheless, "nearly everyone I know in Gaza has contemplated suicide more than once." They suspected that "God's hell, no matter what, would be better than the hell Gaza now is." That was before the current war.

The worse conditions became, the less foreign governments cared. Neither the Trump nor the Biden administration even pretended to pressure Israel to end settlement growth or lift Gaza's blockade. Arab regimes that for decades had refused to recognize Israel absent a solution to the Palestinian question reversed course and signed the Abraham Accords. "Palestinians have lost faith in the efficacy of nonviolent protest," noted the Palestinian American political scientist Dana El Kurd, "as well as the possible role of the international community."

IT WOULD BE simplistic to claim that Hamas launched the October 7 attack because Palestinians had lost faith that nonviolence could improve their lives. Hamas does not poll Palestinians before it kills Israelis. As we have seen, it launched suicide bombings during the early Oslo years, when most Palestinians opposed violence. But as the scholar Richard Davis has documented, Hamas does grow more emboldened when Palestinian support for armed resistance rises. And so while America and Israel's relentless quashing of more peaceful Palestinian initiatives did not cause the October 7 massacre, it reduced the political constraints to carrying it out. In justifying the attack, the Hamas commander Mohammed Deif specifically cited the failure of Palestinian efforts to ensure Israel's compliance with international law. "In light of the orgy of occupation and its denial of international laws and resolutions, and in light of American and Western support and international silence," he declared, "we've decided to put an end to all this."

These dynamics are not unique to Palestinians. Across the world, the political scientist Kirssa Cline Ryckman has noted, the failure of peaceful protest "can encourage the use of violence by convincing demonstrators that nonviolence will fail to achieve meaningful concessions." While there is a crucial moral difference between Hamas's purposeful targeting of civilians and attacks by the African National Congress (ANC) in apartheid South Africa, which were largely restricted to military and industrial sites, the repression of nonviolent tactics encouraged armed resistance there too. "It was only when all else had failed, when all channels of peaceful protest had been barred to us that the decision was made to embark on violent forms of political struggle," declared Nelson Mandela in 1964. He could no longer "continue preaching peace and non-violence at a time when the government met our peaceful demands with force."

Mandela was acknowledging a truth that the poet W. H. Auden said even schoolchildren know: "Those to whom evil is done / Do evil in return." But in the case of Israel, many Jews claim not to know, because that would require acknowledging that evil resides not only in our enemies—Haman, Amalek, Hamas—but in us and the state that speaks in our name.

So, the violence a Jewish state commits against Palestinians breeds more violence against Jews. Muhammad Shehada tells the story of his best friend, Ali, whom he calls "the most thoughtful, most intelligent, most honest, most cultured, and sophisticated person I know."

The two young men debated everything from Ukraine to Jordan Peterson to Jimmy Fallon. Ali held particularly strong opinions about Hamas. He "resented them with every bone in his body for years; he literally couldn't stand them and always criticized everything they did, including their armed actions." He was appalled by the massacre on October 7.

But the war Israel launched in response forced Ali's family to relocate three times within Gaza City. He described having to walk through miles of rubble-filled streets to flee from one heavily bombed neighborhood to another while occasionally hearing screams for help from under bombed homes—noises that got loudest at night.

Eventually, Ali and his family walked south across the Strip, past decomposing bodies, to the city of Deir al-Balah, where they rented a small room for an exorbitant price. Ali spent several hours every day, while bombs fell, searching for food or water. "If there's an afterlife and a judgment day," he told Muhammad, "the only punishment I'll ask from God for the Israelis would be to force them to go out, struggle to find water, and then carry those water gallons for a dozen kilometers every day under air strikes."

In January, Ali was killed by an Israeli missile while walking next to Deir al-Balah's Al-Aqsa hospital.

Before he died, he told Muhammad that he had changed his mind about killing Israelis. In order to deter Israel, he now supported armed attacks.

3

Ways of Not Seeing

On October 13, 2023, the former Israeli prime minister Naftali Bennett appeared on Britain's Sky News. Four days earlier, Israel's defense minister had announced "a complete siege on the Gaza Strip. There will be no electricity, no food, no fuel, everything is closed." The television anchor asked about the closure's effects on vulnerable Palestinians. "What about those in hospital who are on life support and babies in incubators?" he queried. Bennett was incredulous. "Are you seriously going to keep asking me about Palestinian civilians?" he responded. "What is wrong with you? Have you not seen what's happened? We're fighting Nazis."

Within months, Palestinians in Gaza were starving. On March 9, the *New York Times* columnist Nicholas Kristof printed a message from a linguistics scholar in Gaza named Mohammed Alshannat. "Me and my wife have decided to eat a meal every two days just to keep our kids alive as long as we can," he explained. "What is left for us is hay. We have started grinding it, bake it [*sic*] and eat it." On March 18, the Integrated Food Security Phase Classification, a global initiative that collaborates with institutions like the U.S. Agency for International Development, the European Union, and the United Nations Children's Fund (UNICEF) to assess food scarcity, announced, "Famine is imminent as 1.1 million people, half of Gaza, experience catastrophic food insecurity." On March 22, a UNICEF official who had just returned from Gaza reported, "The depth of the horror surpasses our ability to describe it."

Israeli officials denied it all. "There's no imminent famine," the strategic affairs minister, Ron Dermer, told National Public Radio on March 26. "That's a complete lie and fabrication." On April 4, Israel's minister of economy and industry, Nir Barkat, appeared on MSNBC. Asked whether he was "concerned about the human suffering inside Gaza," Barkat simply ignored the question. "We're concerned about the 134 hostages," he replied. "These girls are under tunnels for half a year. Raped, tortured, this is what we're concerned about. We're concerned about those victims in Israel."

Logically, Barkat's response made little sense since the safety of the hostages and the safety of Palestinians in Gaza were intertwined. The war imperiled them both. The vast majority of freed hostages had been released not through military operations but through a November agreement to pause the fighting and trade Israeli captives for Palestinian prisoners. Once released, several former hostages said their greatest fear while in captivity was Israeli bombs. One said it was seeing Israelis protesting for a cease-fire on television that gave him hope he would survive.

But while incoherent as a guide to policy, Barkat's refusal to discuss Palestinian suffering served a psychological purpose. Along with other Jewish leaders, he gave us permission not to care. After traveling to Israel roughly nine months into the war, the Israeli-born Holocaust historian Omer Bartov noted that "people's eyes glaze over whenever one mentions the suffering of Palestinian civilians." What I witnessed in the United States was less extreme, but unnerving, nonetheless. Again and again, I heard rabbis, educators, and ordinary people speak at Jewish communal events about the Israelis killed and abducted on that horrific day. They described their personalities, their jobs, their hobbies, their family histories, the people they loved—their humanity. The exhortations were solemn, fervent, and sometimes left me in tears. They captured a deep truth about what it means to be a Jew, famously expressed in the Talmudic instruction that "all Jews are responsible for each other."

Largely absent was Judaism's other voice, expressed in another famous Talmudic verse, which explains that God created Adam so one "person will not say to another: My father is greater than your father"—my lineage makes me superior to you. In those wartime gatherings I saw Judaism redefined as a purely tribal creed. "We are responsible for each other" became "we are responsible for each other, alone." Often, Palestinian deaths went unmentioned. When they were, it was as a faceless mass. I sometimes heard expressions of sadness that innocent people had died. But I never heard any of the dead described as individuals with their own stories, and personalities, and families they loved. I never heard a name. The message was unmistakable: our lives matter in a way that theirs do not.

Dead Palestinians were statistics. And it was important

that the statistics not be too high. "The 'Gaza Health Ministry' or 'Palestinian Health Ministry in Gaza' is controlled by
Hamas, and the information it releases cannot be trusted,"
declared AIPAC in November. The death figures coming
from Gaza, added Michael Oren in April, are "simply untrue."
Reports that many of the dead were children constituted "a
blood libel," which drew upon "classic antisemitic tropes"
about Jews murdering Christian children. Unlike Bennett,
Dermer, and Barkat, Oren did not refuse to speak about dead
Palestinians. But his essential message was the same: the real
victims are Jews.

There's nothing wrong with caution about death tolls
published in the midst of a war. But it's telling that the Jewish officials who disputed the numbers coming out of Gaza
expressed no similar suspicion of Israel's claims about the Palestinians it killed. It was as if a Jewish state, by its very nature,
were more trustworthy. But when it comes to casualty figures
in Gaza, that's clearly false. Outside experts overwhelmingly
find the Gaza Health Ministry's data far more credible than
Israel's. The reason is simple: the ministry has a practice of
releasing the names of the people it says have died, along with
other identifying information. Israel does not.

For this reason, both the U.S. State Department and the
United Nations have relied on the Health Ministry's data
in the past. After October 7, they did so again. In the first
five weeks of the war, the Health Ministry's total casualty
figures—which came from hospital morgues—were endorsed
by U.S. officials, the UN, the World Health Organization, and
Human Rights Watch. In the most in-depth public analysis
to date of the ministry's reporting from the beginning of the

war, researchers at the U.K. nonprofit Airwars painstakingly verified close to three thousand civilian deaths from the first seventeen days of the conflict. They found that, if anything, the ministry's numbers were too low: only 75 percent of the names they verified had made it onto the official casualty list.

As the war continued, however, Israel destroyed or damaged most of Gaza's hospitals, leaving many unable to effectively identify and report the dead from their morgues. As a result, the Health Ministry said it was forced to resort to simple head counts by the hospitals' spokespeople, and only months later did it slowly begin to recover identifying information from families, once death certificates had been issued. By the end of March, around a third of its reported fatalities were unidentified. The irony is hard to miss: the percentage of unidentified casualties rapidly rose—making it easier for Israel's supporters to deride the ministry—because of Israel's own actions. Still, at no point were the ministry's overall figures far from Israel's. By the end of April, the Health Ministry concluded that almost thirty-five thousand Palestinians had been killed. In early May, Netanyahu put the number at thirty thousand. In January, the Israeli journalist Yuval Abraham reported that the Israeli army considered the Health Ministry's total casualty numbers so reliable that it frequently cited them in its internal briefings.

It is harder to know how many of the dead are civilians. Scholars from the London School of Hygiene and Tropical Medicine who analyzed the Health Ministry's data determined that 68 percent of those killed in the first several weeks of the war were women, children, or the elderly. Since most adult men are not Hamas fighters, the percentage of civilians was certainly higher than that. But in later months, communication from the ministry became more chaotic. In March, it was still reporting that women and children made up more than 70 percent of casualties—a figure derived from Gaza's government media office rather than the ministry's own tallies. That number is probably too high. Michael Spagat, a University of London economist who specializes in measuring war deaths, estimated in May that of the casualties the Health Ministry had managed to identify, women, children, and the elderly constituted around 60 percent. But he still found the data coming out of Gaza far more dependable than Israel's. In May, in an interview with the TV personality Dr. Phil, Netanyahu alleged that almost half of the people Israel had killed were "terrorists." How he determined that is anyone's guess. "It's a bit rich of them to be criticizing the figures released by the Hamas-controlled this and that," Spagat told the *Toronto Star*, "and then they just float numbers out of thin air."

BY THE END of August, the Gaza Health Ministry had closed the gap and managed to identify over 80 percent of reported fatalities, with records showing that one-third of the identified dead were under the age of eighteen. That's more than 11,350 children—with the real number even higher because many have not been identified or even reported, and because Gaza's health authorities do not include children who have died from malnutrition and disease. That's at least thirty-four Palestinian children—more than an entire classroom—killed on average every single day since October 7. Of the dead children whose names we know, over seven hundred were under the age of one. These are the realities whose public discussion Oren deemed a "blood libel."

In addition to minimizing the human toll of Israel's war, Jewish leaders shifted the blame. "Hamas is responsible for getting Palestinian civilians killed," declared AIPAC on October 14. The reason: it uses them as "human shields." In lobbying materials it distributed in the war's first eight months, the organization employed the phrase at least sixteen times.

The human shields argument piles fallacy upon fallacy. Under international law, using civilians as human shields means forcing them to live alongside military targets. It doesn't mean fighting in an area that just happens to have civilians around. Hamas certainly does the latter. It fights from within Gaza's population, and thus puts civilians at risk. But that's typical of insurgent groups. No guerrilla force puts on brightly colored uniforms, walks into an open field, and takes on a vastly more powerful conventional army. "From the American Revolution and the Italian Risorgimento to anti-colonial struggles in Malaya, India, Sri Lanka and Vietnam as well as Algeria, Angola and Palestine, militants have hidden among civilians," notes the Israeli-born international law professor Neve Gordon. "Hamas, in this sense, is no outlier."

In fact, even conventional armies often operate near civilians. The Israeli military locates its headquarters in central Tel Aviv. Twenty-four schools sit within a kilometer and a half of its General Staff building, which houses the offices of its top commanders. Because such intermingling is common, international law is clear: Civilians don't become fair game just because there are fighters nearby. In the words of the

Additional Protocol to the Fourth Geneva Convention, the presence of fighters in an area "shall not release the Parties to the conflict from their legal obligations with respect to the civilian population." One key legal obligation is proportionality. According to the Additional Protocol, the "loss of civilian life" from an attack cannot be "excessive in relation to the concrete and direct military advantage anticipated."

Israel's assault on Gaza became excessive on October 9, when it cut off food and electricity to everyone in the Strip. The following day, Israel's defense minister announced that he had "released all the restraints" on how Israel fought, and its military spokesman declared that "the emphasis is on damage and not on accuracy." An investigation by the publications +972 *Magazine* and *Local Call* found that in the first five days of fighting alone, Israel bombed more than a thousand "power targets"—which included high-rise apartment buildings, banks, universities, and government offices—that it struck not because of their military value but merely for psychological effect. Israeli officials hoped the destruction would shock Gaza's population into turning against Hamas. Justifying this by invoking "human shields" torches the core principles of international law.

While the human shield argument blamed Hamas for Palestinian deaths, another rationalization blamed Palestinians as a whole. "Remember that the citizens of Gaza, these innocent civilians who so many people are shedding tears about, they voted for Hamas," declared Alan Dershowitz, one of Israel's best-known American defenders. Morton Klein, head of the Zionist Organization of America, cited Hamas's victory as proof that "Hamas overwhelmingly represents the Palestinian people."

Their evidence is the 2006 Palestinian legislative elections, in which Hamas won a majority of the seats. But like fictitious death tolls and human shields, this argument collapses at the slightest pressure. For one thing, the 2006 elections weren't held only in Gaza; Palestinians in the West Bank and East Jerusalem voted too. By Dershowitz's and Klein's logic, that makes them fair game as well. For another, Hamas didn't win a majority of the vote in that election; it won 44 percent. By some accounts, it garnered the bulk of the legislative seats only because candidates from Fatah, its main rival, ran as independents in certain districts, thus splitting the anti-Hamas vote. Are the people being starved and bombed in Gaza today responsible for that? Moreover, Khalil Shikaki's exit polls show that the two issues that most attracted voters to Hamas were the Palestinian Authority's corruption and its inability to maintain law and order. In 2006, more than 60 percent of Hamas voters even said they supported the two-state solution. It takes quite a moral leap to make those voters responsible for a massacre seventeen years later. It takes an even greater leap to blame the Palestinians in Gaza today. For one thing, polls conducted in Gaza just before October 7 found that Hamas was quite unpopular there. For another, only about one-quarter of the Palestinians currently living in Gaza were even old enough to vote in 2006.

In addition to denial and rationalization, there was one final exculpation: Everybody does it. Israeli officials were particularly fond of analogizing its bombing to the United

States' and Britain's wars against the Islamic State in Iraq and Syria (ISIS) and against Nazi Germany. "In any combat situation, like when the United States was leading a coalition to get ISIS out of Mosul, there were civilian casualties," argued the Israeli spokesman Mark Regev in late October 2023. At a press conference a few days later, Netanyahu compared Israel's killing of civilians in Gaza to a British raid on Gestapo headquarters that accidentally hit a children's hospital. "You didn't tell the allies don't stamp out Nazism because of such tragic consequences," he told reporters.

U.S. officials contested the ISIS comparison. They noted that during even the heaviest fighting against the Islamic State, the United States generally dropped two thousand to three thousand munitions per month. In the first month of the Gaza war, Israel dropped ten thousand. But that misses the point. The ISIS and Nazi comparisons aim to render any rate of bombing—any number of civilian deaths—acceptable. When fighting enemies intent on creating totalitarian empires, you do whatever you need to do. But whether or not that was an appropriate attitude to take against Hitler's Germany and the Islamic State, the problem with the Gaza analogy is that Germans in 1944 and Iraqis and Syrians in 2015 were not under foreign occupation. They were members of sovereign states.

That's also why it's misleading to justify Israel's response to October 7 by imagining how the United States would answer an attack by Mexico. The United States doesn't occupy Mexico. It doesn't determine whether Mexicans can import soap and export furniture. When you enter Mexico, border officials don't look up your name in an American government database to determine if you're legally allowed in. Israel exercises that control over Gaza. A better analogy would be America's response to attacks from Indian reservations in the nineteenth century. In Gaza, Israel isn't fighting citizens of another country. It's fighting people who hold no citizenship because Israel forced them from their land and now confines them in a coastal ghetto. It's hard to find contemporary analogies for that kind of war because it's a throwback to the colonial age.

LURKING UNDERNEATH all these arguments is a deeper one: Israel has no choice. Even many Jews who are pained, even horrified, by Gaza's suffering, still can't imagine an alternative. Despite their anguish, they support the war because they believe Israelis will never be safe unless Israel destroys Hamas.

The problem with this logic is that Israel can't destroy Hamas, at least not by force of arms. Don't take it from me. Eight months into the war, the spokesman for the Israel Defense Forces said so himself. As Israeli forces returned yet again to fight Hamas in parts of Gaza from which the group had supposedly been eliminated, Rear Admiral Daniel Hagari admitted, "This business of destroying Hamas, making Hamas disappear—it's simply throwing sand in the eyes of the public."

Israel can't destroy Hamas for the same reason the United States couldn't destroy the Vietcong or the Taliban, the French couldn't defeat the National Liberation Front in Algeria, and the British couldn't defeat the Irish Republican Army (IRA) in Northern Ireland. Insurgents fight from within the civilian population. Defeating them thus requires denying them public support. It requires convincing people who live among the rebels that if they turn against them—at considerable personal risk—they'll get something better in return. When those people live under foreign occupation, it requires convincing them there's a better way of achieving their freedom.

Why would any Palestinian believe that? They look at the West Bank and see that even when Palestinian leaders help Israel repress Hamas, Israel's occupation only grows more entrenched and more brutal. They look at Israel itself and see that barely anyone in the Jewish political mainstream believes they deserve citizenship, either in their own sovereign country or in a single, equal one. In July 2024, when the Knesset held a vote on Palestinian statehood, not a single member from a Jewish party voted yes. Palestinians notice that Israel still imprisons Marwan Barghouti, Hamas's most formidable political rival, a man who has praised Nelson Mandela for his capacity to "defy hatred and to choose justice over vengeance." Because although Barghouti might offer Palestinians a compelling, non-Islamist alternative to Hamas, he still demands Palestinian freedom.

When Israel tells Palestinians they'll remain subjugated no matter what they do, no military campaign against Hamas offers any chance of lasting success. Like U.S. leaders in Vietnam, who endlessly cited body counts of dead Vietcong to show they were winning the war, Netanyahu can boast about how many Hamas brigades Israel has eliminated and how many Hamas rockets it has blown up. But Hamas will recruit more fighters and build more rockets. Just look at the record. Since Hamas took over Gaza in 2007, Israel has

treated it as a military problem, and Hamas has only got-
ten militarily stronger. In 2008, Hamas's longest-range rocket
traveled 25 miles. After a decade and a half of a blockade, and
repeated Israeli bombardments—all aimed at ensuring that
Hamas lacked the weaponry to threaten Israel—Hamas has
launched rockets in this war that can travel 155 miles. Some
of its rockets are assembled from ordnance dropped on Gaza
by Israel. In the 1990s, Hamas boasted roughly ten thousand
fighters. By October 7, it had as many as forty thousand.

Israel can depose Hamas from power in Gaza, as the
United States deposed the Taliban in Afghanistan. But some
close observers think Hamas would actually prefer to operate
as a purely guerrilla force. It will happily relinquish responsibility for picking up the garbage. It understands that no
replacement government will enjoy the slightest credibility if
Israel puts it in power. And Hamas has seen its own popularity grow since this war began, especially in the West Bank. It
also knows that Israel's unprecedented slaughter will provide
it with an unprecedented recruitment bonanza as more shattered people than ever before seek to avenge their dead.

Israeli and American Jewish officials can fantasize about
a world without Hamas. But even if the organization did
somehow disappear, some other armed group would simply take its place. Palestinians, after all, have been fighting
against Zionism, and later Israel, for roughly a century. The
Arab revolt of 1936–39, the Battle of Karameh in 1968, the
airline hijackings of the 1970s—none of them were carried
out by Hamas because Hamas wasn't even created until 1987.
Palestinian resistance long predates Hamas and would surely
postdate it too. And the more brutally Israel behaves, the

more brutal that resistance is likely to be. As Ami Ayalon, the former head of Shin Bet, Israel's domestic security service, has warned, "If we continue to dish out humiliation and despair, the popularity of Hamas will grow. And if we manage to push Hamas from power, we'll get al-Qaeda. And after al-Qaeda, ISIS, and after ISIS, God only knows."

The problem with supporting Gaza's destruction because you think Israel needs to destroy Hamas is that, as grave as Hamas's crimes have been, Israel doesn't have a Hamas problem. It has a Palestinian problem. Its problem is that Israeli security and Palestinian security are interconnected. Which means it's foolish to think that Israel grows safer when it reduces Gaza to rubble. Because if people in Gaza aren't safe, they will sooner or later ensure that Israelis aren't either.

THE INSISTENCE THAT Israel must destroy Hamas, even as it becomes ever more obvious that it can't, is ultimately just another way of not facing the human consequences of this war. It's another way of not seeing what is being done in our name. It's not all that different from the claim that the Gaza Health Ministry invents Palestinian deaths or that Hamas bears the blame for those deaths because it uses Palestinians as shields, or that what Israel is doing in Gaza is no different from what the Allies did in World War II. These claims don't withstand even modest scrutiny. They're less arguments than talismans. They ward off dangerous emotions like grief and shame. During Vietnam, Rabbi Abraham Joshua Heschel said, "Whenever I open the prayer book I see before me images of children burning from napalm." I suspect that's what we fear: that if we put down our amulets and look Gaza in the eye, we'll never get its images out of our head. We'll look at our prayer books, many of which include prayers for the army that killed Muhammad's friend Ali, and see Gaza's burning, starving flesh. We'll see it on the walls of our synagogues and Jewish Community Centers, at our Passover seders and Shabbat meals. The ground underneath us will grow unsteady.

Maybe we'll even fear the judgment of God. Heschel did. "God's voice is shaking heaven and earth, and man does not hear the faintest sound," he told an antiwar meeting in 1968. "The Lord roars like a lion. His word is like fire, like a hammer breaking rocks to pieces. And people go about unmoved, undisturbed, unaware." If you consider those fears nonsensical, then rest easy: console yourself that there is no moral accounting, either in this world or in the next. But any Jew who thinks Heschel was right to tremble in 1968 should be trembling now.

"It is weird to wake up one morning," noted Heschel during Vietnam, "and find that we have been placed in an insane asylum." One way of illustrating the insanity of mainstream Jewish discourse about Gaza is to imagine how Jews would react if another country, another people, made the arguments we make regularly about this war.

When other governments kill civilians, they contest the casualty figures too. In 2011, the UN accused the Syrian regime of killing more than four thousand people in its crackdown against antigovernment protests. Syria's leader, Bashar al-Assad, insisted the figures were false. "Who said that the United Nations is a credible institution?" he asked. Sound familiar? In 2015, when UN and U.S. officials accused

Saudi Arabia of bombings that killed dozens of noncombatants in Yemen, the Saudi foreign minister said the critics "need to be careful about facts and fiction." A year later, when international monitoring groups charged that America's war against ISIS had killed more than fifteen hundred civilians, a Pentagon spokesperson derided the claims as "propaganda." Would most Jews trust these denials? Of course not. We'd recognize that governments—democratic, authoritarian, and everything in between—try to minimize their crimes.

Governments also blame someone else. Do we think Israel invented the alibi of human shields? In 2017, *Arab News,* a newspaper owned by the Saudi government, accused Riyadh's opponents in Yemen of "the use of civilians as human shields" because their "forces are still concentrated in residential areas." In 2022, four days after Moscow sent its troops to capture Kyiv, the spokesperson for Russia's Defense Ministry said Ukraine's government "uses the residents of the city as a 'human shield' for the nationalists who have deployed artillery units and military equipment in residential areas." During Vietnam, the U.S. military dropped leaflets alleging that the communist Vietcong "use defenseless women and children as shields." And where did many Vietcong fighters hide as U.S. bombs rained down on Vietnamese civilians? In a vast labyrinth of underground tunnels, just like Hamas. Because if you're a guerrilla force being pummeled by one of the strongest air forces in the world, that's a logical thing to do.

Would the Jews who today invoke human shields to blame Hamas for Israel's bombs fault the Vietcong for America's bombs or Ukraine for Russia's? Not a chance.

If any other government faced the accusations being leveled against Israel by journalists, academics, diplomats, human rights groups, international courts, the United Nations—and by the population being killed—most Jews would believe them. In the 1990s, the American Jewish Committee supported the international tribunals that tried the leaders of Rwanda and the former Yugoslavia. In February 2024, Jonathan Greenblatt condemned the "genocide of the Uyghur people in China." How did the AJC and ADL decide that these regimes were doing something wrong? By listening to the same human rights groups that they call antisemitic when they condemn Israel. While some Jews on the religious right, especially in Israel, mock the entire concept of human rights as Western and therefore un-Jewish, that's not the way most Jewish leaders speak. It's certainly not how they speak to the world. When asked in May 2024 about the warrant for his arrest recommended by the prosecutor of the International Criminal Court, Netanyahu didn't denounce the concept of war crimes tribunals. He said they should target Iran and Syria. He didn't reject the ICC's legitimacy. He just wants it to investigate someone else. He claims to believe in international law. Just not for the Jewish state.

This Jewish exceptionalism grants Israel license to disregard the entire world. Just over a month into the Gaza war, Yossi Klein Halevi, one of Israel's most influential English-language political commentators, published an essay arguing that Israelis "find ourselves at a moral disconnect with much of the international community." He did not answer this disconnect by rebutting any of the moral criticisms leveled at Israel's conduct—its blockade of humanitarian supplies, its leveling of entire neighborhoods, its mass killing of children. He did not even answer the strategic criticism: that Israel cannot defeat Hamas without offering Palestinians some hope that their oppression will end. Instead, he told a story. Halevi asserted that during the second intifada, when Israel was rebuffing international criticism, the UN secretary-general at the time, Kofi Annan, asked, "Can the whole world be wrong and only Israel is right?" Israelis, according to Halevi, "unhesitatingly replied: Absolutely." That, Halevi explained, should be Israel's response to criticism over Gaza. Tell the world to go to hell.

The Israeli government has done exactly that. On May 26, two days after the International Court of Justice ordered Israel to halt its offensive in the southern Gaza city of Rafah, Israel bombed Palestinians sheltering there in tents. The bomb ignited a fire that killed 45 people and injured almost 250. A doctor at the hospital that received the wounded said, "Many of the dead bodies were severely burned, had amputated limbs and were torn to pieces." Netanyahu's response? The following day he cited a woman named Ilana Buskila whose daughter was murdered on October 7 and who said she wanted Hamas destroyed. "One thousand prosecutors at The Hague cannot stand even for a second against this pure truth pronounced by Ilana Buskila," Netanyahu insisted, "against the justness of our moral path."

Such statements can best be understood as a kind of theology. Israel is righteous by definition. Its war in Gaza remains moral even when its crimes are documented for all to see. More than sixty years ago, Hannah Arendt warned that Jewish nationalism contained this danger. "The greatness of this people was once that it believed in God," she wrote in 1963. "And now this people believes only in itself?" That's the real meaning of Netanyahu's words. When he proudly declares that a Jewish state cannot be judged by any external standard, he is making that state—and the Jewish people for whom it speaks—an object of worship. And, as in the Bible, idolatry usually accompanies other sins. You "raise your eyes toward your fetishes, and you shed blood," the prophet Ezekiel rebuked the Israelites in the sixth century BCE. "You have committed abominations." He could have been speaking about this war.

4

The New New Antisemitism

The Anti-Defamation League, the American Jewish Committee, and the Israeli government are all active on X, the social media platform formerly known as Twitter. Between October 7, 2023, and June 4, 2024, the ADL's and AJC's X accounts, and the official accounts of the Israeli government and Israeli prime minister, used the word "starvation" or "famine" fewer than ten times. They used the word "antisemitism" more than a thousand times.

For establishment Jewish organizations that want to avoid looking closely at what Israel has done in Gaza, accusing Israel's critics of antisemitism is the single best way to avert one's eyes. It's more effective than questioning death tolls, invoking human shields, or comparing Israel's bombing to other wars, because those arguments require discussing Gaza. Accusations of antisemitism change the subject entirely. They turn a conversation about the war into a conversation about the motives of the people who oppose it.

This doesn't mean antisemitism isn't dangerous. It's among the most resilient and destructive forms of hatred in history.

The British scholar David Feldman compares antisemitism to an ancient "reservoir" of hostile ideas about Jews that have "built up over centuries, even over millennia." Because Jews have for so long been depicted as cunning, malevolent, and all-powerful, anti-Jewish motifs offer a cultural depository, which people draw from—sometimes unconsciously, sometimes deliberately—when trying to explain phenomena that enrage or bewilder them. Parents alarmed by the coarsening of American culture notice that Hollywood is filled with left-wing, atheistic Jews. Donald Trump's closing advertisement in the 2016 presidential campaign just happens, while denouncing the "global power structure that is responsible for the economic decisions that have robbed our working class," to feature an image of Lloyd Blankfein, who runs an investment bank named Goldman Sachs. A Pittsburgh man obsessed with Central American asylum seekers decides that their journey to the United States is being masterminded by the Hebrew Immigrant Aid Society (HIAS). And when he learns that a local synagogue participates in HIAS's National Refugee Shabbat, he makes it the target of his fury.

This tendency to invest Jews, Jewish initiatives, and Jewish ideologies with demonic, superhuman powers can also shape criticism of Israel and Zionism. On August 4, 2024, after protesters in Venezuela flooded the streets to protest dictator Nicolas Maduro's electoral fraud, he blamed the unrest on "the communication power of Zionism, which controls all the social networks, the satellites and all the power." That same day, after violent anti-immigrant riots erupted across the United Kingdom, a tweet claiming "The 'State of Israel' is burning down the UK" garnered one million views.

. . .

BUT IT'S CRUCIAL to distinguish condemnations of Israel and Zionism that deploy antisemitic concepts from the condemnation of Israel and Zionism itself, which is no more bigoted than opposing any other state or political ideology. Israeli and American Jewish leaders constantly conflate the two. They deploy charges of antisemitism to try to silence criticism of a war whose morality they can't defend. They claim it's bigoted to propose replacing Jewish supremacy with equality under the law. And in their zeal to defend Israel, they often ally with far-right politicians whose white Christian nationalism threatens Jews.

It wasn't always this way. In the first two decades of Israel's existence, its diplomats tried to discredit foreign critics. But America's most influential Jewish groups didn't always play along. They were far warier than they are today of hurling accusations of antisemitism at Israel's detractors.

The American Jewish establishment viewed antisemitism differently because it viewed its mission differently. In the mid-twentieth century, American Jewish organizations were more focused on the struggle for civil rights than on defending the Jewish state. That orientation led them to describe antisemitism as intertwined with other forms of bigotry. Groups like the ADL and AJC, notes the historian Peter Novick, focused on "the common psychological roots of all forms of prejudice" and "consistently minimized differences between different targets of discrimination." If various forms of prejudice were interconnected, then fighting racism against Blacks was a good way to fight antisemitism against Jews.

Underlying this view was the assumption that bigotry—

whether espoused by Tsar Nicholas I, Heinrich Himmler, or George Wallace—was stronger on the ideological right. Conservatives tend to revere the good old days, or at least their imagination of them. In Germany, the Nazis had peddled myths of a glorious, racially pure past. In the postwar United States, segregationists and nativists defended an older, less inclusive vision of America. So, while establishment Jewish leaders rejected communism, they viewed liberals—who championed progress—as better allies for themselves and other historically marginalized groups.

To this day, most other organizations representing traditionally oppressed American communities take this view. The NAACP sees anti-Black racism as a bigger problem among conservative Republicans than among progressive Democrats. That's also how the National Organization for Women views sexism, the Mexican American Legal Defense and Educational Fund views discrimination against Hispanics, and the Human Rights Campaign views homophobia and transphobia. These groups recognize that progressives are capable of bigotry, of course. But they also recognize that conservatives are far more likely to romanticize earlier periods in American history, when white straight Christian men were more comfortably in charge. That's why Donald Trump vows to Make America Great Again.

But in the late 1960s and early 1970s, the American Jewish establishment began to abandon that view. The Civil Rights and Voting Rights Acts had passed. A younger, more militant group of Black activists was more wary of alliances with whites. American Jews—who for decades had pursued integration into the broader society—were starting to worry that assimilation threatened Jewish identity. And in this moment of political transition, the 1967 war—which pitted Israel against Egypt, Syria, and Jordan—hit American Jews with seismic force. The fear that Israel might be destroyed, followed by its stunning victory—in an almost biblical six days—catapulted Zionism to the center of institutional American Jewish life. American Jewish groups raised $100 million for Israel in a single month. After the war, the American Jewish Committee began sending its staff to a summer training program in the Jewish state. "The Six-Day War of 1967," argues the historian Steven T. Rosenthal, "transformed Israel into an object of secular veneration."

But this created a problem. While American Jews were rallying around Israel like never before, some on the left were embracing the Palestinian cause as part of a global anticolonial struggle. In 1967, two influential Black activist groups, the Student Nonviolent Coordinating Committee (SNCC) and the Black Panthers, along with a leader of the New Left organization Students for a Democratic Society, all condemned Israel. In 1973, the United Nations General Assembly—led by newly decolonized states in the global South—decried "zionism [*sic*] and Israeli imperialism."

By the early 1970s, the American Jewish community's traditional view of antisemitism—that like other bigotries it emanated mostly from the right—was in direct conflict with its desire to defend Israel, many of whose fiercest critics now hailed from the left. So, a new understanding of antisemitism—designed to shield Israel—was born. It remains with us to this day.

In 1974, Arnold Forster and Benjamin Epstein, two officials at the Anti-Defamation League, published a book titled *The New Anti-Semitism*. What made it new, they argued, was that Jew-hatred, long associated with the far right, was now ideologically ambidextrous. It was just as dangerous on the far left. Since the mid-1960s, the authors asserted, "the Radical Left" had abandoned "traditional left-wing opposition to anti-Semitism and today represents a danger to world Jewry at least equal to the danger on the right."

Forster and Epstein weren't wrong to see antisemitism on the global left. Employing age-old stereotypes about Jews' omnipotence and financial acumen, leftists sometimes make Jews—or Zionism—a stand-in for all the evils of global capitalism or imperialism. In the 1960s and 1970s, much of this rhetoric emanated from the USSR. Soviet leaders and their Eastern European clients had been accusing local Jews of being Zionist agents since the early 1950s. But the propaganda grew more intense after Moscow cut diplomatic ties with Israel following the 1967 war. When antigovernment protests rocked Poland in 1968, party officials blamed the "international Zionist mafia." That same year, when Czechs launched the experiment in liberalization known as the Prague Spring, Soviet newspapers called the reformers "agents of [an] . . . international Zionist organization." Even leftists who didn't take orders from Moscow sometimes talked about Zionists in the same classically antisemitic way that people have long talked about Jews. In 1967, for instance, SNCC attacked the "Zionist controlled press" and claimed that the Rothschilds, who "CONTROL MUCH OF AFRICA'S MINERAL WEALTH," had been instrumental in Israel's creation.

The problem with Forster and Epstein's argument was that they didn't merely acknowledge that leftists sometimes deployed antisemitic tropes. They described the left's anti-Zionism as antisemitic in and of itself—as if only Jew-hatred could explain why people opposed to colonialism and racism might oppose an ideology that consigned Palestinians to legal inferiority and a state that after 1967 held millions of Palestinians under military law.

But Forster and Epstein's argument caught on. In the half a century since its publication, Jewish leaders have again and again warned of a "new antisemitism," generated by an alleged surge of left-wing Jew-hatred. And as the scholars Adam Haber and Matylda Figlerowicz have noted, it usually coincides with growing support for Palestinian rights.

Even before October 7, anxiety about a "new antisemitism" was again on the rise. Since 2009, when Netanyahu returned to power, Israel had been governed by right-wing governments hostile to a Palestinian state. Polls suggested that American progressives—especially younger ones—were growing more critical of Israel. And although they enjoyed little power in Washington, anti-Zionist organizations like Students for Justice in Palestine (SJP), Jewish Voice for Peace (JVP), and the Council on American-Islamic Relations (CAIR) were making inroads on the activist left. For pro-Israel groups, all this added up to a new wave of leftist antisemitism. In 2022, the ADL's Jonathan Greenblatt denounced SJP, JVP, and CAIR by name. "These groups," he argued, "epitomize the Radical Left, the photo inverse of the Extreme Right that ADL long has tracked." It was the same argument his predecessors had made half a century earlier:

Antisemitism now constituted as grave a threat on the left as on the right.

After decades of repetition, the "new antisemitism" thesis has become conventional wisdom. Jewish officials, journalists, and politicians routinely insist that antisemitism constitutes as serious a problem among progressives as among conservatives. But academic research doesn't generally support this. It tends to confirm the older view that American Jewish groups held in the 1950s and 1960s: antisemitism—like many other forms of bigotry—is much higher among conservatives. In 2022, two political scientists, Eitan Hersh and Laura Royden, published the most comprehensive study ever of the relationship between Americans' views about politics and their views about Jews. They found that "antisemitic views are far more common on the right than on the left."

In a direct refutation of the "new antisemitism" thesis, Hersh and Royden showed that the vast majority of progressives distinguish their feelings about Israel from their feelings about American Jews. The researchers actually invited progressives to link the two but didn't find many takers: "Even when primed with information that most U.S. Jews have favorable views toward Israel—a country disfavored by the ideological left—respondents on the left rarely support statements such as that Jews have too much power or should be boycotted." Hersh and Royden didn't claim there is no relationship between antisemitism and anti-Zionism. But they noted that the Americans who supported punishing American Jews for Israel's actions were far more likely to reside on the ideological right.

In 2019 and 2020, researchers at UCLA reached a similar

conclusion. They asked hundreds of thousands of Americans about both their attitudes toward Jews and their position on military aid to Israel. Republicans who opposed military aid held more negative views of Jews than those who supported it. But among Democrats, there was barely any correlation. Democrats who opposed arms sales to Israel were roughly as favorably inclined toward Jews as Democrats who supported them. Among progressives, opinions about U.S. policy toward the Jewish state and opinions about Jews did not go hand in hand.

In Europe as well, research suggests that antisemitism is higher among conservatives. A 2018 study of attitudes toward Jewish immigration in twenty European countries noted that while Muslims held more negative views of Jews than non-Muslims, antisemitism was far higher on the right than on the left. A 2021 study of sixteen European nations found that the single best predictor of antisemitism was xenophobia. The Europeans with the most negative views of Arabs, Africans, and Muslims also held the most negative views of Jews.

This doesn't mean people who are anti-Israel can't also be anti-Jewish. As the Hersh and Royden and UCLA studies suggest, right-wing antipathy to Israel—the kind once associated with Pat Buchanan and David Duke and now championed by white nationalists like Nick Fuentes—is frequently antisemitic. And while progressives are less likely to hold anti-Jewish views than conservatives, their critiques of Israel still sometimes deploy the kind of antisemitic tropes used by Maduro and SNCC.

One such trope is that Jews are disloyal to the nations in which we live. We care only about our own. The Hersh and

Royden study found that roughly 20 percent of Americans believe American Jews are more loyal to Israel than they are to the United States. This identification of Jews with Israel helps explain why antisemitic incidents tend to spike around the world when Israel's actions produce a global outcry. Three separate studies conducted between 2001 and 2014— one in Belgium, one in Australia, and one in the United States—all found a clear correlation: when Israel kills more Palestinians, Jews around the world report more discrimination and abuse.

On a massive scale, this is what happened after October 7. In the nearly four months between October 7 and January 30, the FBI opened three times as many investigations into hate crimes against Jews as it opened in the four months preceding the attack. I got a glimpse of this upsurge when I spoke in early 2024 at a liberal arts college where sentiment ran strongly against the war. Several Jewish students told me they feared being ostracized if they openly supported Israel. In and of itself, such ideological intolerance doesn't constitute antisemitism. A Christian or even Muslim student who vocally supported Israel would likely have been treated the same way. But one young man recounted being called a Zionist because he had worn a kippa, which showed how the line between anti-Zionism and antisemitism can blur. A fellow student associated him with Israel because he was a Jew.

THE RISE IN ANTISEMITISM after October 7 was part of an ugly tradition not only in Jewish history but in American history. When Americans grow hostile to a foreign government or movement, they often blame Americans who share an ethnicity or religion with the overseas actor they despise. German Americans were terrorized during World War I. Japanese Americans were interned during World War II. Muslim Americans were persecuted after September 11. Chinese and other Asian Americans were assaulted during COVID. And while some Americans after October 7 took out their anger at Israel on American Jews, others took out their anger at Hamas on Palestinian, Arab, and Muslim Americans.

The media generally missed these historical parallels because Israel—unlike Germany during World War I, Japan during World War II, or China today—is America's ally. But it's an ally that's strongly disliked by a segment of the U.S. population. As Hersh and Royden discovered in a separate study, young, left-leaning Americans view Israel as negatively as they view Russia and Iran. Antipathy to Israel is rarer on the right, but it exists, and is more often rooted in antisemitism. So, Jews have become the latest in a long line of Americans to suffer because we are associated with a foreign country that some other Americans hate.

The answer to such bigotry should be clear: Americans are not responsible for foreign governments or organizations just because they have a common ancestry. There was nothing inherent in being German American in the 1910s that made you a supporter of the kaiser's Germany and nothing inherent in being Japanese American in the 1940s that made you a supporter of imperial Japan. Similarly, there is nothing inherent in being Chinese American today that makes you favor the People's Republic of China or in being Palestinian American that makes you approve of Hamas. Supporting foreign governments or organizations is a political choice, not an intrinsic expression of one's ethnic or religious identity.

This distinction is crucial to combating antisemitism that is connected to anger at Israel. We must demand that Israel's detractors clearly distinguish between a foreign country and their fellow Jewish citizens. But we must also make that distinction ourselves. And for the most part, Jewish leaders don't. In establishment American Jewish circles, supporting Israel is depicted not as a political choice but as an inherent part of being a Jew. "Zionism is fundamental to Judaism," the ADL's Greenblatt declared in November 2023. The following April, at a hearing on antisemitism on college campuses, Representative Kathy Manning, the former chair of the Jewish Federations of North America, referenced "the central role Israel plays in Judaism." These statements aren't only incoherent—Judaism existed for millennia before the Zionist movement and the State of Israel were born—they're also dangerous. It's precisely because Judaism and the State of Israel are separate that Jews should not be blamed for Israel's actions. By Greenblatt's and Manning's logic, there's no difference between writing "Free Palestine" on the walls of an Israeli embassy and writing it on the walls of a synagogue because they are both, in their essence, Zionist institutions. Jews are never responsible for antisemitism. We are, however, responsible for fighting it wisely. And conflating Israel and Judaism does exactly the opposite.

But if conflating Israel and Judaism is a terrible way to defend Jews, it's an effective way to discredit Palestinians because it turns Palestinian opposition to Zionism from a natural response to oppression into a form of bigotry.

During the Gaza war, no group has worked harder to depict Palestinians and their supporters as bigots than the ADL. It recorded more than twice as many antisemitic incidents in 2023 as occurred the year before. A majority of the ADL's examples don't involve Israel—a swastika in a school bathroom, for instance—and some of those that do involve Israel are clearly antisemitic. For instance, the ADL reported that shortly after October 7, someone yelled, "Fuck the Jews, Free Palestine" at visibly Jewish people in Washington, D.C. who were walking home on Shabbat.

Yet many of the Israel-related incidents that the ADL calls antisemitic are not directed at Jews per se. Forty-two percent of them involve anti-Zionist rhetoric expressed after October 7. One of the slogans the ADL cites most often is "From the river to the sea, Palestine will be free," which it deems "an antisemitic charge denying the Jewish right to self-determination, including through the removal of Jews from their ancestral homeland." Israel's foreign minister equates it to a "call for the genocide of the Jewish people in Israel."

Many Palestinian scholars deny that. They maintain that the slogan evokes the democratic vision that Palestinian nationalists championed before the PLO accepted dividing the land into two states. In 1970, for instance, Fatah, the PLO's most influential party, released a series of essays that envisioned one "democratic state in Palestine"—from the river to the sea—yet rejected expelling Jews and proposed making both Hebrew and Arabic official languages. Congresswoman Rashida Tlaib, whom the House of Representatives censured for using the phrase, calls it "an aspirational call for freedom, human rights, and peaceful coexistence."

The expression clearly means different things to different people. A March 2024 University of Chicago poll found that 66 percent of American Jewish college students—but only 14 percent of Muslim students—interpret it to mean that "Palestinians should replace Israelis in the territory, even if it means the expulsion or genocide of Israeli Jews." There's no way to prove who's right. But the best way to try would be to simply ask the people who use the phrase. As far as I know, neither the ADL nor any other pro-Israel organization has ever done that. And in a certain sense, they don't care. Even if activists overwhelmingly endorsed Tlaib's vision of a Palestine based on equality and peaceful coexistence, it wouldn't change their thinking. For Jewish leaders in the United States and Israel, it's axiomatic that without a Jewish state, Israeli Jews can't be safe.

What makes the ADL's antipathy to the phrase "river to the sea" so ironic is that there already is a country that extends from the Mediterranean to the Jordan. Israeli leaders use similar expressions, all the time, to describe the territory they rule. The founding charter of Netanyahu's Likud Party declares, "Between the Sea and the Jordan there will be only Israeli sovereignty." And while the ADL can speculate about how a Palestinian state from the river to the sea would treat Jews, Israel's treatment of Palestinians isn't hypothetical. Israel was created by displacing roughly 750,000 Palestinians in 1948, and it displaced several hundred thousand more in 1967, when it extended its borders from the river to the sea. Most of the Palestinians under Israeli control lack citizenship, and none enjoy legal equality. Israel now stands accused of genocide at the International Court of Justice, a charge endorsed by some of the most prominent human rights lawyers in the world.

Between the river and the sea, in other words, Israel has already perpetrated, or is perpetrating, the very abuses that the ADL and the Israeli Foreign Ministry accuse Palestinian activists of wanting to perpetrate. It's a remarkable act of projection. But it serves a purpose. Labeling the slogan antisemitic—even genocidally antisemitic—turns public attention away from how Israel is treating Palestinians now, especially in Gaza, and redirects attention toward how Palestinians might treat Jews were they in charge. It replaces the actual subjugation that Palestinians experience as an oppressed people with the theoretical subjugation that Jews might experience were the shoe on the other foot.

There's a similar double standard on the question of violence. In its catalog of antisemitic incidents, the ADL includes slogans that contain the word "resistance" or "intifada." For instance, "When people are occupied, resistance is justified" or "Long live the intifada."

Like "river to the sea," these phrases are ambiguous. Resistance can be armed or unarmed. Even if armed, it can respect international law or violate it since people under occupation—be they in Ukraine or the West Bank—have the right to militarily resist foreign armies but not to target civilians. Similarly, intifada means uprising. It does not mean uprising against Jews; it means uprising against anyone. It's the word Arabic newspapers used for the protests in Paris in 1968 and Egypt in 2011. According to the Arabic-language website of the United States Holocaust Memorial Museum, the Arabic word for the Warsaw Ghetto uprising is "intifada."

There have been two Palestinian intifadas against Israel. The first, in the late 1980s, was largely unarmed. During the second, in the early 2000s, Palestinian fighters killed one thousand Israelis in suicide bombings and other attacks.

The ambiguity of these terms is a problem. The aftermath of October 7 was an extremely inopportune time for slogans that blur the line between different forms of resistance. After Hamas fighters purposely murdered, maimed, abducted, and sexually assaulted civilians, I wish more pro-Palestinian activists had clearly committed themselves to the rules of war. I wish they had acknowledged that, morally, not all intifadas are the same.

This refusal to acknowledge that Jewish Israelis deserve the protections of international law constitutes a form of dehumanization. If Jewish Israelis are settlers because their state displaced a native population, then so are Americans, Canadians, Australians, Argentines, and many others. If only Jewish Israeli civilians forfeit their right to life for that sin, that's antisemitism.

But if it's wrong to endorse violence against Israeli civilians, then endorsing violence against Palestinian civilians is wrong too. Given what Israel has done to Gaza, pro-Israel slogans like "Israel has the right to defend itself" and "I stand with the IDF" are at least as ominous as "intifada" or "resistance is justified." Yet Jewish leaders have no problem with those. Some Jews say the acid test of whether a chant like "river to the sea" or "intifada" is threatening is whether most Jews think it is. But if that's the standard, then why shouldn't Palestinians determine whether pro-Israel slogans threaten them?

. . .

THE DOUBLE STANDARD ISN'T accidental. The whole point of conflating anti-Zionism with antisemitism is to depict Palestinians and their supporters as bigots, thus turning a conversation about the oppression of Palestinians into a conversation about the oppression of Jews.

Consider the way Jewish leaders talk about America's campuses. In April 2024, Netanyahu alleged that "antisemitic mobs have taken over leading universities." He claimed that "they attack Jewish students; they attack Jewish faculty. This is reminiscent of what happened in German universities in the 1930s."

There have indeed been attacks on Jews on U.S. campuses. A May 2024 study by Hillel International found that 17 percent of Jewish students said they had been verbally harassed as a result of pro-Palestinian protests and 7 percent said they had been physically assaulted. At Cornell, a student threatened to stab and rape his Jewish classmates. At the University of Georgia, a Jewish student was attacked by someone who said, "You Israeli, I am going to murder you and all your family." While being asked if they were Jewish, two Ohio State students were assaulted outside a bar.

My kids are close to the ages of those students, and they make their Jewishness visible in many ways. In an era of rising antisemitism, I naturally worry for their safety. But Netanyahu's depiction of American universities is still absurd. It's absurd because although Israel has become deeply unpopular among the progressive students whom he deems an antisemitic mob, the data is clear: the vast majority of campus progressives distinguish between Jews and Israel. When Hersh surveyed college students in February 2024, he found the same pattern that he and Laura Royden had observed in the country as a whole: considerable antisemitism on the right; very little on the left. "A sizeable minority of young adults on the right endorses statements that are explicitly prejudicial against Jews," Hersh noted. But "hardly anyone on the left agrees." Despite their often negative views of Israel, only roughly 5 percent of left-wing students agreed that "all Israeli civilians should be considered legitimate targets of Hamas."

The University of Chicago study reached the same conclusion. It found that while college students were three times as likely as Americans as a whole to oppose Zionism, they were actually less likely to affirm antisemitic statements like "Jews have too much power" and "when Jews are violently attacked, it is because they deserve it." The authors concluded that "campus anger today is mainly against Israel as a state and not the Jewish people per se."

This doesn't mean Jewish students find campus life easy. For those raised in pro-Israel environments, anti-Zionism can be traumatic even when it doesn't involve animus toward Jews. Hostility to Israel has become so pervasive in progressive circles that Zionist students sometimes feel like ideological pariahs. This hostility doesn't come from nowhere. It's hard to ask Palestinians to care about the feelings of pro-Israel students while Israel slaughters and starves their families. Still, I wish leftist activists more often acknowledged that there's a tradition of cultural Zionism, championed in the mid-twentieth century by figures like Martin Buber and Judah Magnes, which wanted a thriving Jewish culture in Palestine-Israel but opposed a Jewish state. And

I wish leftist activists had more empathy for the historical trauma that leads many young Jews, especially those who are just one generation removed from state-sponsored anti-semitism, to support Zionism even in its statist form. It's no coincidence that some of the most vocal Zionist activists on American campuses are Jews whose parents emigrated from Iran. "Instead of understanding diaspora Zionism and affinity with Israel as residual products of the bludgeoning history meted out to Jews during the twentieth century and earlier," notes the socialist writer Daniel Randall, "much of the left treats them as something akin to a mortal sin." That's not the way leftists generally treat members of other minority groups raised to hold exclusionary and illiberal beliefs. One rarely hears of South Asian students barred from their campus environmental or LGBTQ group because they sympathize with Prime Minister Narendra Modi's virulently anti-Muslim brand of Hindu nationalism. Treating Zionist students as pariahs is both unfair and counterproductive. The best way to convince Jewish students that their safety does not require Jewish supremacy is not to stigmatize them. It's to talk to them.

But Zionist students must be willing to listen, even when it's painful. They must distinguish between being made uncomfortable and being made unsafe. When I speak on campus, I often notice a pattern: The Jewish students who have spent the most time listening to Palestinians—by taking classes on Palestinian history, attending events with Palestinian speakers, or simply getting to know their Palestinian classmates—are the least likely to equate anti-Zionism with antisemitism. These interactions help them understand why

Palestinians and their supporters might dislike Israel without disliking Jews.

In so doing, they also gain empathy for the Palestinian and pro-Palestinian students whom Netanyahu and the ADL demonize. Because the dark irony of Netanyahu's claim that American universities resemble German universities during the Third Reich is that the students and faculty in greatest danger are Palestinians and their supporters. They are routinely punished, silenced, and even beaten, all in the name of keeping Jews safe.

In the weeks and months after October 7, trucks featuring the names and faces of pro-Palestinian activists orbited at least nine universities. In several instances, they showed up outside students' homes. Numerous pro-Palestinian students had job offers withdrawn—all for articulating views that were no more supportive of violence than those routinely expressed by pro-Israel students who supported the war. Pro-Palestinian students were far more likely to be suspended than their pro-Israel counterparts, and their organizations were far more likely to be banned, even in the absence of evidence that they acted more violently. To the contrary, a May 2024 study by the Armed Conflict Location and Event Data Project found that 97 percent of pro-Palestinian protests in the United States since October 7 had been peaceful.

By any measure, in fact, Palestinian and pro-Palestinian students and faculty have endured much more violence than they have inflicted. Pro-Palestinian protesters were sprayed with a nausea-inducing chemical at Columbia in January, in an attack that sent at least ten students to the hospital; beaten with sticks by assailants who tore down their encampment at UCLA in April; and rammed by a car when they protested outside a Columbia trustee's house in May. In April, police broke the ribs of a Palestinian American historian protesting at Washington University in St. Louis. In May, they gashed the head of a Palestinian American sociologist at the University of Wisconsin.

In perhaps the greatest irony of all, some of the pro-Palestinian activists who suffered this violence and repression were Jews. At Dartmouth, police zip-tied a former chair of the Jewish studies program and threw her to the ground when she filmed them arresting students at a pro-Palestinian encampment. Columbia suspended its chapter of the anti-Zionist group Jewish Voice for Peace. The ADL responded by commending Dartmouth's president for summoning law enforcement and congratulating Columbia's president for her work "to protect Jewish students"—even though she had just suspended an organization composed of Jewish students. It was the logical corollary of Greenblatt's insistence that Zionism and Jewishness are inseparable: Reject Zionism and you're no longer a Jew. You're an honorary Palestinian, and thus capable only of menacing Jews, not of being menaced yourself. Your safety becomes dispensable.

That's even truer for actual Palestinians, especially in Gaza. The Strip has college students itself—lots of them. Education is among the few things Gazans can control, and they devote themselves to it fervently. Zaher Kuhail, the founder and former president of Gaza's University of Palestine, told the newspaper *Le Monde*, "We built academic infrastructures with our sweat, blood and donations." Despite Gaza's immense poverty, college students make up 4 percent of its population, roughly the same percentage as in the U.K.

In justifying Columbia's suspension of JVP, the ADL declared on November 10, "Tactics of intimidation have no place on campus." Several days earlier, Israel had launched its second assault on Gaza's Al-Azhar University. Videos showed its buildings enveloped by massive clouds of smoke. By February, according to UNESCO, Israel had damaged twelve institutions of higher learning in Gaza.

In April 2024, *The New York Times* contacted members of the 2023 graduating class from Al-Azhar's dental school. Two of them, Aseel Taya and Noor Yaghi, had been killed by Israeli air strikes. Madeha Alshayyah's sister was missing; her grandmother lay dead beneath rubble. Ola Salama's uncle's body had been found with no head or feet after Israel bombed his house. Mazen Alwahidi had lost forty-six pounds and was eating donkey feed. Noor Shehada was surviving on wild herbs. Rabeha Nabeel and her family had been displaced five times and eventually returned to their home to find it without walls. Areej al-Astal had managed to give birth despite being so short on food that she gained no weight during her pregnancy. More than one hundred members of her extended family were dead. "The word 'dreams' has ended," she told the *Times*. "It no longer exists in our imagination."

Between them, the X accounts of the Anti-Defamation League, the American Jewish Committee, the Israeli government, and the Israeli prime minister mentioned college students more than four hundred times between October 7, 2023, and June 4, 2024. Not once did they mention the suffering of students in the Gaza Strip.

5

Korach's Children

We are the children of Korach. He appears in the book of Numbers, once the Israelites' journey through the desert has already gone seriously wrong. He assembles a band of rebels against Moses and his brother, Aaron, and accuses them of elitism. "All the community are holy, all of them, and God is in their midst," Korach proclaims. "Why then do you raise yourselves above God's congregation?" Moses responds by preparing a test. To see who enjoys divine favor, he offers incense to God and has the rebels do the same. God appears and the earth swallows Korach whole. Contest over.

But the question remains: What did Korach do wrong? There are many opinions. But the one that should haunt us comes from Yeshayahu Leibowitz, the iconoclastic Orthodox social critic whom the philosopher Isaiah Berlin called "the conscience of Israel." Leibowitz focused on Korach's use of the word "holy." He noted that four verses earlier God had told Moses to tell the Israelites "to observe all My commandments and to be holy to your God." Holiness was conditional; it depended on keeping the commandments. Korach, by contrast, said the Israelites were already holy. It wasn't a standard they needed to meet. It was inherent in who they were.

What made Korach's argument so dangerous, Leibowitz argued, was that it corrupted another key concept in the Hebrew Bible: chosenness. For Leibowitz, it was essential that being chosen by God did not make Jews better than anyone else. It meant they had a special set of obligations—to follow the Torah's commandments—not a special set of virtues. In the Bible, the prophets do not tell the Jewish people they can do no wrong. They tell them that it is precisely because they have a unique relationship with God that their wrongs can never be excused. "You alone have I singled out of all the families of the earth," says the prophet Amos, in God's name. "Therefore, I will call you to account for your sins."

But Amos wouldn't have needed to say that had Korach's message not been so seductive. Who wouldn't be tempted by the claim that chosenness—sometimes called election— makes you holy no matter what? Rabbi Shai Held, a prominent contemporary theologian, notes that "the prophets were constantly forced to fight against interpretations of election that guaranteed the people impunity and rendered them impervious to critique." Since the beginning, some Jews have wanted to place us above the law.

Leibowitz believed that Korach's heresy echoed throughout Jewish history. He traced it through the eleventh-century Spanish poet and philosopher Yehuda Halevi, the sixteenth-century rabbi known as the Maharal of Prague, and elements of Chasidic thought that date from eighteenth-century Poland and Ukraine. Scholars can debate whether these disparate figures and movements make up a coherent

ideological lineage and how much support their view has in
the Torah itself. But even if Leibowitz was right that Jewish
exceptionalism constituted a persistent and deviant strain in
medieval and early modern Jewish thought, it couldn't do
much damage. So what if a few dreamers in Moorish Spain
or the Silesian shtetl consoled themselves with the idea that
deep within us lies a special spark of the divine? They didn't
have the power to do anything about it.

All that changed with the creation of Israel. Only once
Jews control a state—with life-and-death power over millions of non-Jews—does Korach's claim of intrinsic Jewish
sanctity became truly dangerous.

To understand why, it's worth remembering that the Bible
considers states—which in its time meant kingdoms—very
perilous things. While they may be necessary to avoid chaos,
they can easily become instruments of oppression. When
the Israelite elders ask the prophet Samuel for a king, God
instructs him to both grant their wish and list the many cru-
elties a monarch will inflict.

Kings are most dangerous when they view themselves
the way Korach viewed the Israelites: as inherently holy and
thus infallible. When they see themselves as gods. In Jewish
tradition, the preeminent example of this is Pharaoh, whose
despotism is inseparable from his belief that he is divine. The
Bible tries to prevent Jewish Pharaohs by insisting that Jewish kings are entirely mortal. Their authority does not come
from any innate superiority. It stems from their willingness
to follow God's law. In the book of Deuteronomy, Moses tells
the people that a Jewish king must commission the writing
of a Torah scroll and "observe faithfully every word of this

Teaching as well as these laws. Thus, he will not act haughtily toward his fellows." The Talmud says the difference between a good and a bad king is that the former both "judges and is judged."

We no longer live in an age of Jewish kings. Yet Leibowitz's nightmare has come true: Many Jews treat a Jewish state the way the Bible feared Jewish monarchs would treat themselves: as a higher power, beholden to no external standard. Again and again, we are ordered to accept a Jewish state's "right to exist." But the language is perverse. In Jewish tradition, states have no inherent value. States are not created in the image of God; human beings are. States are mere instruments. They can protect human flourishing, or they can destroy it. If they do the latter, they should be reconstituted to make them more respectful of human life. The legitimacy of a Jewish state—like the holiness of the Jewish people—is conditional on how it behaves. It is subject to law, not a law in and of itself.

Critics might counter that there is a vast difference between condemning Korach for implying that the Jewish people can disregard God's law and condemning Israel because it disregards international laws established by imperfect human institutions like the United Nations and the International Criminal Court. It's a fair point. The specific standards by which Israel should be judged are subject to reasonable debate. But there must be a standard. When it comes to Israel's treatment of all the people under its control, half of whom are Palestinian, Jews must have some fixed principle that allows us to say, "This goes too far." The loyalty we feel to each other, sometimes described as *ahavat yisrael*, cannot offer Israel unlimited moral license. "*Ahavat yisrael* is not—cannot be—the religious equivalent of 'our country, right or wrong,'" argues Shai Held. "There can be no Jewish theology without a fundamental commitment to human solidarity." If you support a Jewish state no matter what it does to Palestinians, then you're treating it as infallible. You're walking in the footsteps of Korach.

I sometimes imagine asking the people who speak for our community a series of questions: How many Palestinians would Israel have to kill in Gaza before you urged the United States to stop sending it weapons? How many Palestinian prisoners would Israel have to torture and sexually abuse with impunity before you acknowledged the right of international courts to put Israeli leaders on trial? How long must West Bank Palestinians live under military law before you stop calling Israel a democracy? How many human rights groups have to accuse it of apartheid before you question the principle that Jews alone must rule? I've had enough conversations like these to predict the responses. They'd likely include references to Hamas, human shields, Iran, and anti-semitism, coupled with expressions of regret that the cruel realities of the Middle East require Israel to protect itself in such painful ways. But the essential answer would be clear: There is no limit. No matter how many Palestinians die, they do not tip the scales, because the value of a Palestinian is finite and the value of a Jewish state is infinite.

Jewish tradition has a term for investing supreme value in things other than God. It is *avodah zarah,* commonly translated as "idolatry." It is among Judaism's gravest sins, one of only three that we must avoid even at the cost of our lives.

In the Talmud, Rabbi Yochanan calls rejecting idolatry the essence of being a Jew.

It is not idolatrous to support a Jewish state. Leibowitz himself believed that while a Jewish state possessed no "intrinsic value," it could be justified as a means of Jewish self-protection if it ended its occupation of stateless Palestinians in the West Bank and Gaza Strip. He died in 1994, so there's no way of knowing whether he would still hold that view now. But he considered it idolatrous to *worship* a Jewish state, to elevate its value beyond that of the human beings under its control. And that idolatry suffuses contemporary Jewish life.

To grasp its pervasiveness, consider the treatment of those who do not bow down. In most of the Jewish world today, rejecting Jewish statehood is a greater heresy than rejecting Judaism itself. In Israel, there is no religious requirement for election to the Knesset. Of the fourteen prime ministers in Israel's history, only one, Naftali Bennett, has observed Jewish law. But there is a Zionist requirement: political parties cannot oppose "the existence of the State of Israel as a Jewish and democratic state."

Many American Jewish institutions also deem rejecting Jewish statehood the greatest possible sacrilege. Hillel, which serves Jewish college students, declares on its website that "all kinds of students are invited and encouraged to bring their whole selves. Whether students keep kosher or have never attended synagogue; whether they want to participate in Shabbat or in a study group." Synagogue and Shabbat are optional. Israel, however, constitutes "a core element of Jewish life." There the tolerance ends. Speakers who "delegitimize" Jewish statehood are explicitly prohibited from speaking at Hillel. There is no prohibition on speakers who "delegitimize" God.

Treating a state as a god is a very frightening endeavor. It confers upon mortals a level of veneration that we do not deserve and will always abuse. Leibowitz called it "the essence of fascism." It is especially frightening when that state operates along explicitly tribal lines. In a 1963 speech on "religion and race," Abraham Joshua Heschel defined an idol as "any god who is mine but not yours, any god concerned with me but not you." He was critiquing Americans who deified white supremacy. But he could have been talking about Jews who deify Jewish supremacy. Worshipping a country that elevates Jews over Palestinians replaces Judaism's universal God—who makes special demands on Jews but cherishes all people—with a tribal deity that considers Jewish life precious and Palestinian life cheap.

"To act in the spirit of religion," added Heschel, "is to unite what lies apart, to remember that humanity as a whole is God's beloved child. To act in the spirit of race"—or tribal supremacy of any kind—"is to sunder, to slash, to dismember the flesh of living humanity." Heschel wasn't speaking in metaphor. As of September 22, 2024, according to the Gaza Health Ministry, whose overall casualty figures have historically mirrored Israel's, this war has left around 6 percent of Gaza's population injured or dead. That's equivalent to more than 500,000 Israelis or 18 million Americans. If the war ended tomorrow, and Gaza was rebuilt at the same pace as after previous wars, reconstruction would take eighty years. This is idolatry in practice. We have built an altar and thrown an entire society on the flames.

· · ·

THE *KORBANOT*, the religious offerings, extend beyond Gaza. They include Israeli Jews themselves: it may take decades to grasp how gravely this war endangers them. Ziad al-Nakhalah, who at the age of three saw Israel murder his father when it massacred Palestinians in Khan Younis in 1956, currently heads Palestinian Islamic Jihad. Israel has already killed more than one hundred times as many Palestinians in Gaza in this war as it killed back then. How many three-year-olds will still be seeking revenge sixty-nine years from now?

But our Moloch wants more. To defend Israel, American Jews are harming our community and our country. More than half a century ago, the writer I. F. Stone noted that "Israel is creating a kind of moral schizophrenia in world Jewry." Jews whose welfare in our own countries "depends on the maintenance of secular, non-racial, pluralistic societies" were championing a Jewish state "in which the ideal is racial and exclusionist." Today, as progressives turn against Israel, they are forcing American Jews to choose: defend exclusion in Israel or inclusion in the United States. And some of America's leading Jewish institutions are choosing the former.

That choice is making American Jewish life more insular and more repressive. After October 7, the 92nd Street Y, which for decades symbolized New York Jewish cosmopolitanism by hosting writers like James Baldwin, Susan Sontag, and Czesław Miłosz, canceled its annual literary series rather than host writers who boycott Israel. Around the same time, Brandeis University, named for America's most famous Jewish advocate of free speech, banned its chapter of Students for Justice in Palestine and began advertising itself as a campus where students could "feel safe in their Jewish identity" because they wouldn't encounter fierce criticism of Israel. This is self-ghettoization. To avoid an open debate about Israel, some of America's most venerable Jewish institutions are abandoning the intellectual openness in which we once took pride.

Defending Israel at all costs doesn't only threaten American Jewish culture. It threatens American liberty. The right-leaning Zionist Organization of America has endorsed legislation that could defund America's universities—a cornerstone of any free society—if they permit anti-Zionist events on campus. In March 2024, as Donald Trump was securing the Republican nomination for president, the ADL honored his son-in-law Jared Kushner and justified the decision by citing Kushner's work supporting Israel. That same year, AIPAC endorsed more than one hundred Republican congressional candidates who at Trump's behest tried to overturn the 2020 election.

As Stone suggested, Jews in the United States and Europe have long seen open societies as crucial to our safety. But now that authoritarian right-wing parties—from the GOP to France's National Rally to the Alliance for Germany—have become more pro-Israel than their left-leaning competitors, some Jewish leaders are making a different bet: that we can thrive in white Christian ethnostates. This is where our theology of Jewish statehood leads. To defend tribal supremacy in Israel, we're empowering tribal supremacy in the United States and Europe, where we're not even the dominant tribe.

We're also offering up one final sacrifice: international law. To protect Israel, the organized Jewish community—in Israel and across the world—is working to smear and intimidate the world's leading human rights organizations and international courts. In 2022, when Amnesty International concluded that Israel was practicing apartheid, the Anti-Defamation League attacked it for contributing "to intensified antisemitism around the world"—even though Israel's own leading human rights groups had leveled the same charge. A former head of the Mossad, Israel's external security agency, reportedly threatened the then prosecutor of the International Criminal Court and her family when she considered launching an investigation into Israeli war crimes. In 2024, after a new ICC prosecutor did propose such an investigation, AIPAC applauded the House of Representatives for voting to impose sanctions not only on him but on his two sons.

This thuggery degrades the legal system born after World War II and expanded after the genocides in Rwanda and the former Yugoslavia, to restrain the predatory actions of states. It is a gift to Vladimir Putin, Narendra Modi, Xi Jinping, and any other tyrant who worries he may be shamed by human rights groups or prosecuted by the ICC. If Israel can destroy Gaza with impunity, warns Agnès Callamard, Amnesty's secretary-general, it will leave "international law likely in its death throes and nothing yet to take its place save brutalist national interests and sheer greed." In our zeal to protect Israel no matter what, this is the world we're helping to create.

THERE IS another path. But it requires recognizing what Leibowitz taught: that in our capacity for justice and injustice, we are no different from everyone else.

That may not seem like a big conceptual shift. Most Jews

don't walk down the street thinking we are immune from sin. Yet that assumption permeates our communal conversation about Israel: it's always someone else's fault. Israel expels 750,000 Palestinians in 1948: it's because Arab governments told them to leave. Israel occupies millions of West Bank Palestinians who lack citizenship and the right to vote: it's because Palestinians wouldn't accept Israel's peace offers. Human rights groups accuse Israel of practicing apartheid: Why aren't they focused on Syria and Iran? Student protesters demand that Israel stop obliterating Gaza: they're antisemites, or at best, wildly uninformed. The alibis change but the bottom line remains the same: Jews are victims. Israel has done nothing fundamentally wrong.

For generations, Jews in Israel and the diaspora have built our identity around this story of collective victimhood and moral infallibility. For many of us, questioning Jewish statehood means questioning Jewishness. What would being Israeli even mean in a state that didn't favor Jews, given that Jewish favoritism is built into the name "Israel" itself, which is a synonym for the Jewish people? And what would replacing Jewish supremacy with legal equality mean for American Jews when most American synagogues feature an Israeli flag on the *bima* and a prayer for Israel in the liturgy? Remove Jewish statehood from Jewish identity and, for many Jews around the world, it's not clear what is left.

But the benefit of recognizing that Jews are not fundamentally different from other people is that it allows us to learn from their experience. Jewish exceptionalism is less exceptional than we think. We are not the only people to use a story of victimhood to justify supremacy.

In the early twentieth century, Afrikaners dotted South
Africa's landscape with memorials to the concentration camps
into which British troops herded them during the Second
Boer War. We may know nothing of that history and may
consider it trivial compared with our millennia of persecution, but it shaped the way many Afrikaners saw the world.
They believed themselves menaced both locally and globally:
at home, by Black South Africans, who supposedly wanted
them dead, and abroad, by Britain and the rest of the unreli-
able, hypocritical West, which was willing to let it happen.

Today, this narrative may seem delusional and grotesque.
But I spent part of my childhood in apartheid-era Cape
Town: trust me, Afrikaners and most other white South
Africans believed it with all their heart. And it wasn't as different from the story Jews often tell ourselves about Israel
as we might like to believe. When Jews imagine a state that
grants Palestinians equality between the river and the sea,
many envisage the supposed barbarism and dysfunction of
the Middle East descending upon pristine Tel Aviv. White
South Africans, who took an equally dim view of their sur-
roundings, nurtured similar fears. They discussed Nigeria
and Congo with as much dread as Jews today discuss Syria
and Iraq. In this part of the world, they muttered, violence is
endemic, and defenseless minorities don't survive.

They found neighboring Zimbabwe's example particularly
chilling. In 1987, even Helen Suzman, a South African liberal, noted that the transition from white rule there had "cost
20,000 lives." She warned that "the South African transfer
of power will take a good deal more than that." These days,
when people tell me Jews and Palestinians can't live alongside

each other equally because such things aren't possible in the Middle East, my mind flashes back four decades. I remember relatives citing the dictatorships and civil wars north of the Limpopo River as evidence that Blacks and whites couldn't live together in a democratic South Africa. The one group of South Africans I never heard say this were Blacks, just as I rarely hear it from Palestinians today.

White South Africans were just as afraid of being thrown into the sea as Israeli Jews are now. Perhaps more afraid since they constituted a smaller share of the population and had fewer allies overseas. They considered Nelson Mandela's African National Congress a terrorist group, and they weren't alone. It was designated as such by the U.S. government. The ANC's rival, the Pan-Africanist Congress (PAC)—whose unofficial slogan was "one settler, one bullet"—appeared even more menacing. Even Blacks who did not employ violent resistance themselves, like Bishop Desmond Tutu, who in 1984 won the Nobel Peace Prize, were reluctant to condemn it, just as many Palestinians are today. Given these realities, most white South Africans considered it self-evident that without a white army to protect them, their lives would be at grave risk. A 1979 poll found that 84 percent of white South Africans believed "the physical safety of whites would be threatened by black government." White South Africans, noted the journalist Allister Sparks, equated "racial integration with national suicide," just as many Israeli Jews view integration with Palestinians as suicide today.

More than eight thousand miles north of Johannesburg, Protestants in Northern Ireland told a similar story. They justified their dominance with tales of victimhood too. Every

July they waved banners and sang songs about the Siege of
Derry in 1689, when their ancestors starved rather than sub-
mit to a Catholic king, and the Irish Rebellion of 1641, when
Catholics drowned their forefathers in the river Bann. They
too saw themselves as menaced on two fronts. They faced
a local threat: Catholic hordes, who sought to sever Northern Ireland from the United Kingdom and swallow it into
an Ireland that Protestants viewed as almost as backward
and authoritarian as white South Africans viewed Africa and
many Jews today view the Middle East. And they faced the
threat of abandonment from London, which echoed the fears
that white South Africans once had, and Jews have today, of
betrayal by a duplicitous, feckless West.

Northern Ireland's Protestants were terrified of equality. They obsessed over the violence of the Catholic Irish
Republican Army, which they viewed not as a response to
oppression but, in the words of one Irish political scientist,
as "straightforward tribal barbarism." Protestants trembled
when they contemplated what these killers might do if
handed the arsenal of a state. It would be the Siege of Derry
all over again. When the British, Irish, and U.S. governments
pressured Protestants to abandon their political dominance
in the 1998 Good Friday Agreement, their most famous
leader, Ian Paisley, called it a "prelude to genocide."

That's how many white southerners in the United States
talked as well. If Afrikaners had the Boer War and Protestants in Northern Ireland had the Siege of Derry, the South's
victim story was Reconstruction. According to legend, the
South was plundered after the Civil War by a local enemy,
violent Blacks, and a distant one, the federal government in

Washington. During Reconstruction, declared Alabama's governor, George Wallace, in 1963, "the South was set upon." He uttered those words in a speech warning that in the civil rights era white southerners faced oppression from those same malevolent forces again: Blacks who wanted to seize power and the northern liberals who were helping them. Wallace compared the federal government's treatment of whites in Mississippi to the Nazis' treatment of Jews. The analogy was extreme, but the fears underlying it were commonplace. In the mid-twentieth century, most white southerners considered racial equality a monstrous delusion. As the historian Jason Sokol has noted, "They thought in terms of white supremacy or black supremacy: if blacks gained rights, whites would correspondingly 'wear the yoke.'"

Why were those frightened supremacists wrong? Why didn't the comrades of the ANC and PAC storm through neighborhoods like my grandmother's, chanting "one settler, one bullet" and massacring whites, once apartheid fell? Why didn't the IRA lay siege to Protestant neighborhoods in Derry? At its core, the answer is achingly simple: because most people—Black, white, Catholic, Muslim, Palestinian, whatever—don't take up arms lightly. They don't want to kill or be killed. They do it when they feel they have no other choice. When oppressed people gain a voice in government, they gain another way of speaking to those in power, one that doesn't risk their lives. That doesn't make political violence disappear. But it tends to decrease. That's why South Africa didn't endure a bloody fifteen-year guerrilla war like Zimbabwe: because its leaders realized more quickly that the only way to stop a Black uprising was to give Blacks the vote.

It's why rivers of blood don't run in the streets of Alabama. Imagine how much more racial violence there would be in Wallace's home state today had Black southerners not gained the franchise in 1965.

Or consider the fate of a South African practice called the "necklace." It was the ANC's method for punishing collaborators with the apartheid regime. Comrades would hang a tire around the unfortunate's neck, douse it with gasoline, and set it on fire. In 1985, Nelson Mandela's wife, Winnie, one of Black South Africa's most powerful figures, declared, "With our boxes of matches and our necklaces, we shall liberate this country." The ANC would not condemn the practice. White South Africans shuddered as they imagined handing over the country to such people. But "once a nonviolent way of ending apartheid appeared as an alternative," notes the political scientist Mahmood Mamdani, "hardly anyone could be found to champion necklacing the day after." The "necklace" was a brutal response to a brutal system. Once that system disappeared, it did too.

Mamdani's observation that inclusion yields safety is verified by a small mountain of academic research. A 2010 study of 146 instances of ethnic conflict around the world since World War II found that ethnic groups that were excluded from state power were three times as likely to take up arms as those that enjoyed representation in government. In her 2023 book, *Collective Equality,* the Israeli scholar Limor Yehuda notes that countries that practice "political exclusion and structural discrimination" are far more likely to experience "civil wars."

You can see this dynamic even in Israel itself. Every day, Israeli Jews who are deathly afraid of Palestinians in Gaza and the West Bank place themselves in Palestinian hands when they're at their most vulnerable: on the operating table. Palestinian citizens—sometimes called "Arab Israelis"—constitute 25 percent of Israel's doctors, 30 percent of its nurses, and 60 percent of its pharmacists. Yet few Israeli Jews fear they'll be bludgeoned when they enter a hospital or poisoned when they enter a drugstore. Indeed, they don't generally fear violence from Palestinian citizens at all. They don't even fear violence from Palestinian citizens who are Islamic fundamentalists. In 2021, an Islamist party, the United Arab List, actually joined an Israeli coalition government.

Why do Israeli Jews find Palestinian citizens so much less threatening? It's not because Palestinian citizens don't care about being Palestinian. It's not because they don't remember what Israel did to their families in 1948. It's not because they like Zionism. More than anything, it's because they have citizenship. They can vote. So, although they face severe discrimination, they at least have some peaceful and lawful methods for making their voices heard. Compare that with Palestinians in Gaza, who have no legal way to influence the state that bombs and imprisons them. In 2018, when they marched, largely peacefully, to the fence that encloses Gaza, they were simply shot.

Political inclusion doesn't only foster peace within countries. It fosters peace between them. In the 1970s and 1980s, South Africa waged war against five neighboring states that supported the ANC's armed struggle. When that armed struggle ended, the regional wars did too. Today, Jews don't only fear Palestinians; we fear the entire "axis of resistance," which has its headquarters in Iran and branches from Lebanon to Yemen to Iraq. But that axis is Tehran's way of using the Palestinian struggle to amplify its regional power. If the Palestinian struggle ends, so does the central justification for Iran and its allies' "resistance" against Israel. Iran's leaders acknowledged that in 2017, when they signed an Organization of Islamic Cooperation statement endorsing the Arab Peace Initiative, which offered to recognize Israel if it permits a sovereign Palestinian state in the West Bank, Gaza, and East Jerusalem and a "just solution to the Palestinian refugee problem." The message was clear: when Palestinians stop fighting Israel, we will too.

THIS DOESN'T MEAN that once Palestinians gain their freedom, peace will break out across the Middle East. It doesn't even guarantee peace in Israel and Palestine. Political systems that give everyone a voice in government can still be profoundly unjust. South Africa remains hideously unequal. So does the United States. In practice, Northern Ireland's schools are still segregated along religious lines. Democratic political systems can be deeply dysfunctional and highly corrupt: the former South African president Jacob Zuma reportedly tried to funnel billions in government assets to his cronies. And these woes—unfairness, ineptitude, malfeasance—can bring democracy down. They may do so in South Africa. They may do so in the United States. After one system of oppression ends, another can rise. The struggle doesn't end.

A future Palestine-Israel would face all these challenges. It would also face one that the United States and South Africa do not: it has no overarching national identity. White and Black Americans both consider themselves Americans; white and Black South Africans both consider themselves South Africans. That's why neither country's name changed when Blacks gained the right to vote. Israel-Palestine is different. Palestinians and Israeli Jews both want self-determination, yet they are almost certainly too intermingled to be divided by a hard border. There are proposals for addressing this challenge: confederation between a Palestinian and a Jewish state, federation within one binational state, a democratic system—like the one in binational Belgium—that guarantees both communities a voice in major decisions. The details matter, but they matter less than the underlying principles. Wherever they live together, Jews and Palestinians should live under the same law. And they should work to repair the injustices of the past. The Israelis who were made refugees on October 7 should be allowed to go home. And the Palestinians who were made refugees in 1948 should be allowed to go home. Historical wrongs can never be fully undone. But the more sincere the effort, the greater the reconciliation that ensues.

No country fully lives these principles. But even when applied imperfectly, they can create miracles. The most important thing we can learn from white South Africans, white southerners, and Protestants in Northern Ireland is not that abandoning supremacy brings safety. It is that abandoning supremacy offers a chance at liberation. "Many white southerners felt that the civil rights years had removed a great burden from their shoulders," writes Sokol. "The weight of a long and bloody past seemed to be lifting." In 2012, a woman named Linda Ervine launched an unlikely initiative in East Belfast, a part of the city from which Protestants violently cleansed Catholics a century ago. She began teaching the native Irish language that Protestants had long feared would be forced upon them if Catholics took over. In an interview ten years later, she said she couldn't meet the demand. In 1996, in a speech in Cape Town to mark the passing of South Africa's new Constitution, the country's deputy president, Thabo Mbeki, spoke about his nation's heritage. He called himself the descendant of the Xhosa, Bapedi, Zulu, Venda, Sotho, and Nguni kings and chiefs who fought British, Afrikaner, and other European colonizers. No surprise there: Mbeki was Xhosa himself, and the scion of a prominent ANC family. Then he said something mind-bending: "I am the grandchild who lays fresh flowers on the Boer graves" and remembers "concentration camps, destroyed homesteads, a dream in ruins." He was talking about the Second Boer War. He was calling himself an Afrikaner. "Being part of all these people," Mbeki continued, "I am an African."

Thirty miles to the east, at Stellenbosch University, the Afrikaner Oxford, a young lecturer named Wilhelm Verwoerd had reached the same conclusion. "We should take the African bit in the Afrikaner identity much more seriously," he told a British journalist, who came to ask why he had joined the ANC. Why was a foreign reporter canvassing the opinions of an obscure academic? Because of Wilhelm's last name. His grandfather Prime Minister Hendrik Verwoerd is widely regarded as the architect of apartheid.

Although it won't look the same, this kind of liberation is possible for us. We can lift the weight that oppressing Palestinians imposes on Jewish Israelis, and indirectly, on Jews around the world. We don't need to warp the souls of young Israeli Jews by sending them to humiliate men in front of their children and restrain screaming women as bulldozers demolish their homes. We don't need to watch them fly off after their military service for long sojourns in Machu Picchu or Kathmandu, where they try to forget what they've seen and done.

American Jews don't need to search for the hidden anti-semitism in every nineteen-year-old anthropology major, or Lutheran grandmother, who condemns Israel because they can't bear seeing another Palestinian child die. We don't need to get decent people fired—the same people who in the 1960s were protesting Vietnam, in the 1980s were protesting apartheid South Africa, and in the 2000s were protesting the Iraq War—just because this time the U.S.-funded human rights abuses they're challenging are being committed by a Jewish state. We don't have to ally with MAGA thugs because racists are Israel's most reliable friends. We don't have to disfigure our communal institutions by suppressing open debate. We don't have to close off a piece of ourselves and barricade it from our best qualities—kindness, compassion, fairness—because that's the only way we can defend what's being done in our name. We can lay down the burden of seeing ourselves as the perennial victims of a Jew-hating world.

I believe this is possible because our tradition says so. It doesn't only speak about God liberating us from being slaves.

It speaks about God liberating us from being masters. In describing the Jubilee year, the semicentennial occasion when slaves are set free, the book of Leviticus declares, "Proclaim release throughout the land for all its inhabitants." A commentary attributed (perhaps incorrectly) to the eighteenth-century German rabbi Yaakov Yehoshua Falk notes that the last three words are oddly expansive. Since only slaves are being freed, why doesn't the verse say, "Proclaim release throughout the land for all its slaves?" The commentary finds the answer in the Talmud, which declares, "One who acquires a Hebrew slave is like one who acquires a master." Slaveholding makes you a kind of slave. That's why the Jubilee year brings liberty to "all the inhabitants" of the land. By freeing the oppressed, it frees oppressors too.

I've had a small taste of that liberation myself. I grew up believing deeply in the necessity a Jewish state. I remember sitting in my dorm room one night in college, hearing people in the foyer outside condemning Israel, and rushing out to set them straight. I took pride in defending the honor of my people. Despite visiting Israel-Palestine since childhood, I didn't spend any meaningful time with Palestinians there until the fourth decade of my life. I was well into adulthood before I read a book by a Palestinian author or had anything resembling a Palestinian friend.

When those experiences began and then became routine, I was initially surprised by the sophistication, the quirkiness, the sweetness, the normality of the people I met. And then I felt ashamed of my surprise. It was by encountering Palestinians that I realized the depths of the dehumanization I had been carrying inside. And gradually—as the defensiveness and disorientation subsided—I felt myself being remade. Conversation by conversation, Palestinians helped me think differently about what it means to defend my people. They helped me redefine Jewish honor. They changed my understanding of what it means to be a Jew.

I remember talking to a Palestinian from the West Bank who had recently visited a Jewish suburb of Atlanta. He had seen Orthodox Jews walking in clusters down the street and noticed that none of them were armed. You know, he said to me, that's possible here too. If we're not afraid, they don't need to be either.

I remember walking with my then twelve-year-old son through the old market in Hebron, a once thriving thoroughfare made desolate by Israel's restrictions on Palestinian travel. I looked up and saw the netting shopkeepers had constructed overhead to protect them from settler projectiles. The Palestinian friend with whom we walked had been arrested and beaten countless times. He lived with indignities that would have driven me to hatred or despair, or both. Suddenly he disappeared. My fear began to mount. There were only Palestinians around. I remembered what one Israeli acquaintance had told me when I said we were traveling to meet a Palestinian in Hebron: that I had no right to put my child at risk.

Then my friend reemerged. He had ducked into a shop and come out with a Bar Mitzvah present for my son. His true gift, I realize now, wasn't the ceramic pomegranate he bought. It was helping a young Jew grow up without racism and fear. Speaking about the relationship between Black and white Americans, James Baldwin wrote, "We, with love, shall force our brothers to see themselves as they are." That's what Palestinians have done for my family and me.

Maybe this sounds grandiose, but I don't think our transformation as Jews is necessary only for Israel and Palestine. It's necessary for the world. Almost two generations ago, humanity witnessed a new birth of freedom. Mandela walked out of prison, Russia held its first free election, young Germans danced atop the Berlin Wall. Democracy's third wave swept aside tyrants from the Philippines to Chile to Benin. The spirit of that era has long since died. Liberty has been receding for decades. From Putin to Modi to Xi to Trump, thugs dominate the globe, inciting tribal violence while they steal their nations blind. In its unchecked cruelty and unbearable pain, the destruction of Gaza is a symbol of our age.

When South Africa's legal team—Black, white, Afrikaner, Muslim, one a protégé of a Jewish judge on her country's supreme court—charged Israel at the International Court of Justice, it seemed to me that they weren't only trying to end a genocide. They were trying to pass a torch. Imagine a legal team not with Xhosa names like Ngcukaitobi and Afrikaner names like du Plessis but with names like Khalidi and Levy, using Palestine's and Israel's liberation as an example, and as an instrument to seek justice around the globe. What other place on earth could more effectively rouse humanity from its desolation and birth a new age of freedom?

Speaking of Abraham's descendants in the book of Genesis, God says, "All the families of the earth shall bless themselves by you." Perhaps this is what it means for the Jewish people to bless humanity in our time. It means liberating ourselves from supremacy so, as partners with Palestinians, we can help liberate the world.

Acknowledgments

I relied on many people in writing this book. I'm grateful to my agent, the extraordinarily wise and savvy Tina Bennett. It was a privilege to be edited by Jennifer Barth, who again and again urged me to see beyond statistics and expert quotations and write from the heart. I'm indebted to Arielle Angel and Daniel May at *Jewish Currents,* who gave me time off to write this book and who through countless conversations over the years helped me think through its arguments. I'm lucky to teach at the Craig Newmark Graduate School of Journalism at CUNY, under the exceptional leadership of Graciela Mochkofsky and Allison Lichter, and to work with Ken Silverman at the CUNY Graduate Center, and Daniel Kaufman. And I've had the good fortune to be a fellow at the Foundation for Middle East Peace alongside three wonderful people, Lara Friedman, Sarah Anne Minkin, and Kristin McCarthy.

Geoffrey Levin, Raphael Magarik, Derek Penslar, Khalil Sayegh, and Rabbi Chaim Seidler-Feller all gave of their expertise when I had questions about certain subjects in this book. Rabbi Caryn Broitman offered vital assistance in the book's final stages. Sam Bahour, Leonard Benardo, Ethan Leib, Matthew Lindenbaum, Chip Manekin, Mikhael Manekin, Daniel May, David Myers, Kathleen Peratis, Nadia Saah, Rami Sarafa, and Muhammad Shehada all read drafts. So did Lia Na'ama ten Brink and Aron Wander, who served as research assistants, although that vastly understates their role. They didn't just unearth much of the information on which this book relies and translate many documents from Hebrew. They were essential thought partners, often drawing on reservoirs of knowledge that far exceed mine. Whatever failings this book has, they are entirely my own. And they would be far graver without Na'ama and Aron's help.

Most important, I need to thank my family. For my entire life, my mother, Doreen Beinart, has modeled love of the Jewish people. She has also modeled a deep love of family, a tradition that my sister, Jean Stern, carries on. That love has enveloped me for my entire life.

Through the writing of this book, I have relied on my wife Diana's astute advice and unstinting support, as I have throughout our lives together. She has offered it without hesitation, despite bearing the brunt of the anger that my public commentary provokes.

That is also true for our kids, Ezra and Naomi. I first began writing on this subject fifteen years ago, in significant measure because of them, because I feared that Jews of my generation were failing Jews of theirs. We were offering them a definition of Jewish solidarity that made them complicit in oppression. Ezra and Naomi were little back then. Now they're teenagers. They have come of age in Jewish institutions where having me as a father is not always easy. Since

October 7, it's become even harder. I've often winced as they describe navigating relationships made more difficult by my views. Never once have they complained. To the contrary, watching their passion, their intellectual curiosity, and their kindness toward those with whom they disagree has been among my greatest joys.

Hard times reveal people's character. I've never been more grateful for Diana's, Ezra's, and Naomi's than I am now.

Notes

A NOTE TO MY FORMER FRIEND

4 and then die: Babylonian Talmud, Kiddushin 39b.

4 lying in the street: Ibid.

4 utter his name: Jeffrey L. Rubenstein, "Elisha Ben Abuya: Torah and the Sinful Sage," *Journal of Jewish Thought and Philosophy* 7 (1998): 139.

4 "poison of a snake": Jerusalem Talmud, Chagigah 2:1.

4 beyond the pale: Rubenstein, "Elisha Ben Abuya," 139.

4 walk on Shabbat: Jerusalem Talmud, Chagigah 2:1.

4 "violent persecution": Chaim Potok, *The Chosen* (New York: Simon & Schuster, 2016), 207.

PROLOGUE: WE NEED A NEW STORY

7 each other's relatives: Babylonian Talmud, Bava Kamma 109a and Rashi on Bava Kamma 109a, s.v. "*ve-khi yesh lekha adam be-yisrael she-ein lo goʾalim.*"

1 · THEY TRIED TO KILL US, WE SURVIVED, LET'S EAT

11 "display her beauty": Esther 1:11. All translated quotations from the Tanakh are from the Jewish Publication Society (JPS) 1985 translation.

12 "The Jews struck": Esther 9:5.

12 On the thirteenth: Esther 9:16–17.

13 Why is Shavuot: The Torah designates Shavuot as a religious festival on which work is prohibited. Purim and Chanukah, by contrast, are established as festivals later, and one is therefore allowed to work on them.

13 The Talmud blames the Jews: Babylonian Talmud, Megillah 12a.

13 A midrash on: Song of Songs Rabbah 2:8.

13 The Talmud devotes: See Babylonian Talmud, Ta'anit.

14 But the Maccabees didn't disappear: See, for example, Babylonian Talmud, Bava Kamma 82b, Sanhedrin, 19a–b, Yevamot 61a, Kiddushin 66a.

14 Contemporary scholars note: Shai Held, *Judaism Is About Love* (New York: Farrar, Straus and Giroux, 2024), 332–35; Genesis Rabbah 45:1.

15 Some have older relatives: For a beautiful story about the way the Holocaust frames one family's experience of Passover, read Daniella Greenbaum Davis, " 'Once We Were Slaves, Now We Are Free': The Passover Seder in Bergen-Belsen That Shaped My Family," *Tablet,* April 20, 2016.

15 There are still fewer Jews: Adam Taylor, "Has the Global Jewish Population Finally Rebounded from the Holocaust? Not Exactly," *Washington Post,* July 2, 2015; "Jewish Population Rises to 15.7 Million Worldwide in 2023," Jewish Agency for Israel, Sept. 15, 2023, www.jewishagency.org.

16 In February 2024: "5 Facts About the Jewish People's Ancestral Connection to the Land of Israel," American Jewish Committee, February 26, 2024, https://www.ajc.org.

17 "The Jewish people are indigenous": "Why Israel Is Not a Settler Colonial State," American Jewish Committee, accessed July 15, 2024, https://www.ajc.org.

17 In his 1923 essay: Ze'ev Jabotinsky, "The Iron Wall," translated from the Russian, originally published in *Rasviet,* Nov. 4, 1923, en .jabotinsky.org.

17 In 1948, the newly: Benny Morris, *1948* (New Haven, Conn: Yale University Press, 2008), 221.

17 In 1958 he hosted: Rachel Havrelock, *The Joshua Generation: Israeli Occupation and the Bible* (Princeton, N.J.: Princeton University Press, 2020), 7.

18 In 1902, Theodor Herzl: Theodor Herzl, *The Complete Diaries of Theodor Herzl* (New York: Herzl Press and Thomas Yoseloff, 1960), III, p. 1194, quoted in Stephen Halbrook, "The Class Origins of Zionist Ideology," *Journal of Palestine Studies* 2, no. 1 (Fall 1972): 86.

18 In "The Iron Wall": Jabotinsky, "Iron Wall."

18 In a 2019 interview: Isaac Chotiner, "Michael Oren Cuts Short a Conversation About Israel," *New Yorker,* May 11, 2019.

18 AJC pins the blame: "Why Israel Is Not a Settler Colonial State," American Jewish Committee."

18 In his 1993 book: Benjamin Netanyahu, *A Place Among the Nations: Israel and the World* (New York: Bantam Books, 1993), 23, 25, 361.

19 Israeli commentators often argue: See, for instance, Yossi Klein Halevi's comment that "the Israeli ethos is to despise victimhood" in "Debates over Zionism and the Future of the Israeli-Palestinian Conflict," UC Berkeley School of Law, April 29, 2024, circa 22:33 minutes in, www.youtube.com/@UCBerkeleySchoolofLaw, and Tal Becker's declaration in an interview with Dan Senor that "in a way, Zionism or Israel is the refusal to be a victim" in "Call Me Back # 223 | Israeli Independence—with Dr. Tal Becker," *Call Me Back—with Dan Senor,* podcast, May 20, 2024, circa 37:24 minutes in, www.youtube.com/@CallMeBackPodcast.

19 "the Jew of the nations": It appears the phrase "Jew of the nations" was coined by the Hebrew University historian Jacob Talmon in a 1976 essay in *The New Republic* (see Jacob Talmon, "The New Anti-Semitism," *New Republic,* Sept. 18, 1976). With slight variations, it has been used countless times since, including by the ADL's then national director Abraham Foxman in a 2003 inter-

view with CNN, the former Canadian attorney general and former president of the Canadian Jewish Congress Irwin Cotler in 2009, the Israeli writer Yossi Klein Halevi in 2024, and Foxman again in 2024. See "New Poll in European Union Sparks Outrage in Israel," interview by Wolf Blitzer with Abraham Foxman, CNN, Nov. 4, 2003; Irwin Cotler, "Global Antisemitism: Assault on Human Rights" (working paper, Institute for the Study of Global Antisemitism and Policy, New York, 2009), 2, 6; Patrick Kingsley, "Accused of Genocide, Israelis See Reversal of Reality. Palestinians See Justice," *New York Times,* Jan. 12, 2024; Jordana Horn, "Former ADL Head Abe Foxman: 'Israel Has Become the Jew Among the Nations,'" *Times of Israel,* March 7, 2024.

19 "which its founders hoped": Derek Penslar, "Shlomo Sand's *The Invention of the Jewish People* and the End of New History," *Israel Studies* 17, no. 2 (Summer 2012): 157.

19 Consider its account: Benny Morris, *Righteous Victims: A History of the Zionist-Arab Conflict, 1881–2001* (New York: Alfred A. Knopf, 1999), 252.

19 "The Palestinian refugee issue originated": "Backgrounder: Palestinian Refugees," Anti-Defamation League, Sept. 1, 2016, www.adl.org.

19 The problem with this: Rashid Khalidi, *The Iron Cage: The Story of the Palestinian Struggle for Statehood* (Boston: Beacon Press, 2007), 131.

20 depopulated Jaffa and Haifa: On Jaffa, see Itamar Radai, "Jaffa, 1948: The Fall of a City," *Journal of Israeli History* 30, no. 1 (March 2011): 35; on Haifa, see Benny Morris, *The Birth of the Palestinian Refugee Problem Revisited* (Cambridge, U.K.: Cambridge University Press, 2004), 186–87, 209.

20 The war's most notorious: Morris, *Birth of the Palestinian Refugee Problem Revisited,* 239.

20 "It was not the entry": Walid Khalidi, "Why Did the Palestinians Leave, Revisited," *Journal of Palestine Studies* 34, no. 2 (Winter 2005): 48. The article is a reprint of the 1959 original.

20 "Jews pleaded": Netanyahu, *A Place Among the Nations,* 142.

20 A 1948 report: "Migration of Eretz Yisrael Arabs Between December 1, 1947, and June 1, 1948," Akevot Institute, accessed July 17, 2024, www.akevot.org.il. In addition, Walid Khalidi's research found that Arab governments, far from telling Palestinians to leave, urged them to stay. See Khalidi, "Why Did the Palestinians Leave, Revisited." Morris determined that between April and June 1948, Arab action "to promote or stifle the exodus was only of secondary importance" and Zionist military operations proved "the major precipitants to flight." See Morris, *Birth of the Palestinian Refugee Problem Revisited,* 181.

21 Thus, even the state: Morris, *Righteous Victims,* 184.

21 Since Jews lived largely: Walid Khalidi, "Revisiting the UNGA Partition Resolution," *Journal of Palestine Studies* 27, no. 1 (Autumn 1997): 13; Walid Khalidi, "Plan Dalet: Master Plan for the Conquest of Palestine," *Journal of Palestine Studies* 18, no. 1 (Autumn 1988): 4–33.

21 "Only a state with": David Ben-Gurion, speech to senior members of Mapai, Dec. 3, 1947, quoted in Ilan Pappé, *The Ethnic Cleansing of Palestine* (Oxford: One World Publications, 2008), 48.

21 "Ben-Gurion was a transferist": Ari Shavit, "Survival of the Fittest," *Ha'aretz,* Jan. 8, 2004. In a 2016 op-ed, Morris apparently reversed his view, arguing that Israel had not committed ethnic cleansing. He stated, "At no stage of the 1948 war was there a decision by the leadership of the Yishuv or the state to 'expel the Arabs'—neither in the Jewish Agency nor in the Israeli government." At the same time, though, Morris admitted, "It's true that in the 1930s and early '40s David Ben-Gurion and Chaim Weizmann supported the transfer of Arabs from the area of the future Jewish state. . . . It's also true that from a certain point during the war, Ben-Gurion let his officers understand that it was preferable for as few Arabs as possible to remain in the new country, but he never gave them an order . . . [and] [i]t's true that in mid-1948 the new State of Israel adopted a policy of preventing the return of refugees." See Benny Morris, "Israel Conducted No Ethnic Cleansing in 1948," *Ha'aretz,* Oct. 10, 2016.

The Hebrew University historian Daniel Blatman has argued that Morris simply redefined ethnic cleansing rather than substantially revising his initial findings. Blatman also notes that Morris had already withdrawn his charge of ethnic cleansing *before* his 2004 interview with Shavit in his 2000 book, *Correcting a Mistake: Jews and Arabs in Palestine/Israel, 1936–1956,* only to seemingly reaffirm it once more in his endorsement of the 1948 expulsions in the interview. See Daniel Blatman, "Yes, Benny Morris, Israel Did Perpetrate Ethnic Cleansing in 1948," *Ha'aretz,* Oct. 14, 2016.

22 George Orwell famously wrote: George Orwell, "Politics and the English Language," *Horizon* 13, no. 76 (April 1946): 261.

22 Amid the crush of people: "Testimony by Nazmiyya al-Kilani—Safed | *Shahadat Nazmiyya al-Kilani—Safad,*" Zochrot, Feb. 12, 2021, www.youtube.com/@Zochrot; Morris, *Birth of the Palestinian Refugee Problem Revisited,* 229.

23 That fall, Israeli troops: Hisham Zreiq, "The Sons and Daughters of Eilaboun," in *An Oral History of the Palestinian Nakba,* ed. Nahla Abdo and Nur Masalha (London: Zed Books, 2018), 229–35; *The Sons of Eilaboun,* directed by Hisham Zreiq, April 25, 2023.

23 During Israel's war of independence: Walid Khalidi, ed., *All That Remains: The Palestinian Villages Occupied and Depopulated by Israel in 1948* (Beirut: Institute for Palestine Studies, 1992), xxxi–xxxii; Morris, *Birth of the Palestinian Refugee Problem Revisited,* 172, 342.

24 "Denying the Jewish people": Jonathan Greenblatt, "ADL: We're Proud of Our Record Defending Jews—and Muslims," *Forward,* December 16, 2020.

24 "Those who may benefit": Avishai Margalit and Joseph Raz, "National Self-Determination," *Journal of Philosophy* 87, no. 9 (Sept. 1990): 461.

24 "right of self-determination": Robert M. Price, *The Apartheid State in Crisis: Political Transformation in South Africa, 1975–1990* (Oxford: Oxford University Press, 1991), 82.

25 That includes the West Bank: Between 2002 and 2017, according

to then head of the Palestinian Committee of Prisoners' Affairs, Issa Qaraqe, Israel detained at least seventy elected members of the Palestinian parliament. "Khalida Jarrar's Arrest Condemned by Palestinian Groups," Al Jazeera, July 3, 2017. As of April 2024, according to the prisoner advocacy NGO Addameer, Israel was holding seventeen members of parliament. Addameer, April 4, 2024, www.addameer.org.

25 Israel controls Gaza: Maram Humaid, "The Seven Border Crossings of Gaza," Al Jazeera, June 15, 2022.

25 Even at the third, Rafah: According to Tania Hary, executive director of Gisha, an Israeli nonprofit that focuses on freedom of movement for people in Gaza, before October 7, "Israel had a tremendous amount of influence" over what crossed through Rafah "through its security coordination with Egypt." Interview by author, August 21, 2024.

25 Israel even controls: "Gaza Up Close," Gisha, June 28, 2023, www .gisha.org.

25 Inside all this territory: Marwan Muasher, "Jordan's Red-line on Admitting Palestinians Is Unlikely to Change," Carnegie Endowment for International Peace, Nov. 21, 2023, www .carnegieendowment.org.

26 Roughly 70 percent: Omer Yaniv, Netta Haddad, and Yair Assaf-Shapira, "Jerusalem: Facts and Trends 2022," Jerusalem Institute for Policy Research, 2022, www.jerusaleminstitute.org .il; "A world of 8 billion: 'Towards a resilient future Harnessing opportunities and ensuring rights and choices for all,'" Palestinian Central Bureau of Statistics, July 7, 2022, www.pcbs.gov .ps. In East Jerusalem, which Israel also conquered in 1967 but unlike the West Bank and Gaza has formally annexed, Palestinians are not granted Israeli citizenship but can apply for it. As of 2022, approximately 5 percent of Palestinian residents of East Jerusalem had obtained Israeli citizenship. Roughly two-thirds of applications are turned down, and the process is often lengthy. Nir Hasson, "Just 5 Percent of E. Jerusalem Palestinians Received Israeli Citizenship Since 1967," *Ha'aretz,* May 29, 2022.

26 The other 30 percent: Since Israel allows only state-approved clergy to conduct legally sanctioned weddings, Jews can only marry other Jews, Muslims can only marry other Muslims, and Christians can only marry other Christians—unless Israelis wed outside the country, in which case the state approves their foreign nuptials. "Religion and State in Israel," New Family, accessed July 21, 2024, www.newfamily.org.il. In 2022, for the first time, an Israeli court recognized online civil marriages. Daniel Estrin, "A Court in Israel Recognizes Online Civil Marriages as Valid," NPR, Sept. 30, 2022.

26 More than 90 percent: Human Rights Watch, "Israel: Discriminatory Land Policies Hem in Palestinians," May 12, 2020, www.hrw.org; "Response on Behalf of the JNF to Petitions for Order Nisi and Temporary Injunction," Dec. 9, 2004, H. C. 9010 / 04 and 9205 / 04, cited in *Israel and the Palestinian Minority 2004*, ed. Nimer Sultany and Adrian Kirwan, trans. Tzivi Shulman (Haifa: Mada al-Carmel—Arab Center for Applied Social Research, 2005), 51. Cited in Mahmood Mamdani, *Neither Settler nor Native: The Making and Unmaking of Permanent Minorities* (Cambridge, Mass.: Harvard University Press, 2020), 295.

26 a 2013 report: "Land Policy and Planning in Israel—No Space for Arabs?" [in Hebrew], The Israel Democracy Institute, March 21, 2013, https://www.idi.org.il.

27 under international law: "A Threshold Crossed: Israeli Authorities and the Crimes of Apartheid and Persecution," Human Rights Watch, April 27, 2021, www.hrw.org; "Israel's Apartheid Against Palestinians: A Cruel System of Domination and a Crime Against Humanity," Amnesty International, Feb. 1, 2022, www.amnesty.org; "A Regime of Jewish Supremacy from the Jordan River to the Mediterranean Sea: This Is Apartheid," B'Tselem, Jan. 12, 2021, www.btselem.org.

27 an "open-air prison": "Palestinians at the End of 2023," Population and Demographic Statistics, Palestinian Central Bureau of Statistics, March 2024, 28, www.pcbs.gov.ps; Linah Mohammad,

Tinbete Ermyas, and Ailsa Chang, "Half of Gaza's Population Is Under 18. Here's What That Means for the Conflict," NPR, Oct. 18, 2023; "Gaza: Israel's 'Open-Air Prison' at 15," Human Rights Watch, June 14, 2022, www.hrw.org. Gaza is roughly 141 square miles, and New York City is roughly 305 square miles. "Gaza Strip's Size Compared to US Cities in Series of Maps," *Newsweek,* updated Oct. 17, 2023; George Lankevich, "New York City," in *Encyclopaedia Britannica,* updated July 22, 2024, www.britannica.com.

27 Palestinians in the West Bank: "Arbitrary by Default: Palestinian Children in the Israeli Military Court System," Defense for Children International-Palestine, May 31, 2023, www.dci-palestine.org.

27 Confined to overcrowded enclaves: "Discriminatory Zoning and Planning Policies," in "Israel's Apartheid Against Palestinians: A Cruel System of Domination and a Crime Against Humanity," Amnesty International, Feb. 1, 2022, www.amnesty.org.

28 more than 88 percent: Anette Kleiman, charged with Public Enquiries and Freedom of Information Requests, "Re: Planning Law Enforcement Following Amendment 116 to the Planning Law" [in Hebrew], Israeli Ministry of Finance, Oct. 9, 2018.

28 In 2018, Israel demolished: Negev Coexistence Forum for Inequality, "Building Demolition in Negev Bedouin Communities, 2014–2023," infographic shared in private correspondence, April 20, 2024.

28 the Bedouin village of Al-Araqib: Oren Ziv, "Twelve Years After It Was First Destroyed, Al-Araqib Is a Symbol of Determination" [in Hebrew], *Sicha Mekomit* [Local Call], July 26, 2022; Zo Haderekh editorial, "The Village of Al-Araqib in the Negev Was Destroyed for the 223rd Time; MK Atauna: They Will Not Be Able to Evict Us" [in Hebrew], *Zo Haderekh* [This Is the Way], March 22, 2023.

28 "principle of equal citizenship": "Proposed Basic Law: A State for All Its Citizens," 20th Knesset, available online at "Adalah Heads

to Supreme Court After Knesset Speaker, Deputies Nix Legislation of Arab MKs' Bill Declaring Israel 'State of All Its Citizens,'" Adalah, June 11, 2018, www.adalah.org.

28 Israel's Knesset speaker: Jonathan Lis, "Knesset Council Bans Bill to Define Israel as State for All Its Citizens," *Ha'aretz,* June 4, 2018.

28 Like those Palestinian parliamentarians: On its website, Students for Justice for Palestine says, "We promote an agenda grounded in freedom, solidarity, equality, safety, and historical justice." Jewish Voice for Peace declares itself committed to the "values of freedom, justice, and equality for all people." "Our Mission," Students for Justice in Palestine, accessed August 20, 2024, www.nationalsjp.org; "Our Core Values," Jewish Voice for Peace, accessed August 20, 2024, www.jewishvoiceforpeace.org.

28 desire Israel's "annihilation": *Times of Israel* staff and agencies, "Netanyahu Likens US Campus Encampments by 'Antisemitic Mobs' to 1930s Nazi Germany," *Times of Israel,* April 24, 2024.

29 "Israel is the only UN member": David Harris, "High Time to Stop Treating Israel Differently," *Times of Israel,* Dec. 29, 2020.

29 "no other country's existence": "Antisemitism Defined: Double Standards Against the State of Israel," World Jewish Congress, May 4, 2022, www.worldjewishcongress.org.

29 "legitimate physical violence": Max Weber, "The Profession and Vocation of Politics" (1919), in *Political Writings,* ed. Peter Lassman and Ronald Speirs (Cambridge, U.K.: Cambridge University Press, 2010), 310–11.

30 In a 2019 poll: Shmuel Rosner et al., *Annual Assessment of the Situation and Dynamics of the Jewish People, 2019 | 5779: Global Trends and Policy Recommendations Integrated Anti-Semitism Index: Europe and the US Special Chapters: Jewish Creativity and Cultural Outputs,* ed. Barry Geltman, Jewish People Policy Institute, Sept. 16, 2019, www.jppi.org.il.

2 · TO WHOM EVIL IS DONE

33 As explosions boomed: "Lilya Ann—Sderot | Seven10Stories," Seven10Stories, Dec. 12, 2023, www.youtube.com/@Seven10Stories.

34 Seven weeks later: "The Children Who Hid for 14 Hours in a Closet, While Their Parents Were Murdered by Terrorists" [in Hebrew], Channel 13, Oct. 19, 2023, www.youtube.com/@News13; Anna Betts and Katherine Rosman, "After 4-Year-Old Hostage Is Freed, Her Family Breathes a Sigh of Relief," *New York Times,* Nov. 26, 2023.

34 For some Israelis: Julia Frankel, "A Freed Israeli Hostage Relives Horrors of Captivity and Fears for Her Husband, Still Held in Gaza," Associated Press, Jan. 16, 2024; Eli Berlzon and Michal Yaakov Itzhaki, "Freed Hostage Says Life in Gaza Is Like Playing 'Russian Roulette,'" *Financial Review,* Dec. 12, 2023; Keren Marciano, "Something of Me Remains in Gaza: Sharon Aloni-Cunio on 52 Days in Captivity, and the Separation from Her Husband, Who Remained in Captivity" [in Hebrew], *N12,* Dec. 23, 2023; Elad Simchayoff, "52 Days in Captivity: A Conversation with Sharon Aloni-Cunio" [in Hebrew], *One a Day* (podcast), Feb. 1, 2024.

35 had a special impact: Ido Efrati, "People Lived for 50 Years with Dormant Trauma, on the Seventh of October It Erupted" [in Hebrew], *Ha'aretz,* Feb. 22, 2024.

35 The massacre transported: Ronen Tal, "The October 7 Massacre Brings Back Horrific Memories for This Iraqi-Jewish Author," *Ha'aretz,* Dec. 13, 2023.

35 "my real Holocaust": Shira Rubin, "In an Israel Changed by Oct. 7, Holocaust Survivors Find a New Mission," *Washington Post,* May 6, 2024.

36 A letter from Israeli progressives: "Statement on Behalf of Israel-Based Progressives and Peace Activists: Regarding Debates over Recent Events in Our Region," Oct. 16, 2023.

37 a "modern-day pogrom": "Community Letter to University Presidents," Anti-Defamation League, Oct. 12, 2023, www.adl.org.

37 "the new Nazis": "PM Netanyahu Meets with German Chancellor Olaf Scholz," Prime Minister's Office, Oct. 17, 2023, www .gov.il.

37 to "blot out": "Statement by PM Netanyahu," Ministry of Foreign Affairs, Oct. 28, 2023, www.gov.il; Deuteronomy 25:17.

37 "entire Israeli families": "UN Security Council Meets on Israel-Palestine Crisis; Nowhere Safe in Gaza," UN News, Oct. 30, 2023, news.un.org; "Israeli Envoy Wears Yellow Star in Address to UN," Telegraph, Oct. 31, 2023, www.youtube.com/@telegraph.

38 "cruel and monstrous": "MK Boaz Bismuth: There Is No Place for Any Humanitarian Gesture—We Must Wipe Out the Memory of Amalek" [in Hebrew], Channel 7, Oct. 16, 2023, www.inn.co.il.

38 "2 million Nazis": Carrie Keller-Lynn and Jacob Magid, "'There Are 2 Million Nazis' in West Bank, Says Far-Right Finance Minister Smotrich," *Times of Israel,* Nov. 28, 2023.

38 crusaders slaughtered Jewish communities: The prayer is called Av HaRachamim. In most Ashkenazi communities, it is not recited when certain joyous or special occasions fall on Shabbat. After October 7, our synagogue decided to say it every week.

39 "in every generation": Pesach Haggadah, www.sefaria.org.

39 gruesome, pitiless attacks: Philippe Girard, *The Slaves Who Defeated Napoleon: Toussaint Louverture and the Haitian War of Independence, 1801–1804* (Tuscaloosa: University of Alabama Press, 2011), 320–22; Karl Davis, "'Remember Fort Mims': Reinterpreting the Origins of the Creek War," *Journal of the Early Republic* 22, no. 4 (Winter 2002): 631–32; David Anderson, *Histories of the Hanged: The Dirty War in Kenya and the End of Empire* (New York: W. W. Norton, 2005), 119–39.

39 "Every native population": Jabotinsky, "Iron Wall."

40 "the Arabs attacked us": "1929 Riots," Just Vision, www.justvision .org; Martin Buber, "Hans Kohn: Zionism Is Not Judaism," in *A Land of Two Peoples: Martin Buber on Jews and Arabs,* ed. Paul R. Mendes-Flohr (Chicago: University of Chicago Press, 2005), 97–100.

40 "Let us not cast": "Moshe Dayan's Eulogy for Roi Rutenberg—

April 19, 1956," Jewish Virtual Library, www.jewishvirtuallibrary
.org.

40 "In our times": Yeshayahu Leibowitz, "Occupation and Terror"
(1976), in *Judaism, Human Values, and the Jewish State,* 237.

42 "Personal grievances": Basel Saleh, "Palestinian Suicide Bombers
Revisited: A Critique of Current Wisdom," Ideas for Peace, originally published at Peace and Conflict Monitor on Jan. 18, 2005,
www.ideasforpeace.org.

42 "gave up their lives": Robert J. Brym and Bader Araj, "Suicide
Bombing as Strategy and Interaction: The Case of the Second
Intifada," *Social Forces* 84, no. 4 (2006): 1979.

42 "individual-level exposure": Sivan Hirsch-Hoefler et al., "Conflict Will Harden Your Heart: Exposure to Violence, Psychological Distress, and Peace Barriers in Israel and Palestine," *British
Journal of Political Science* 46, no. 4 (2014): 845.

42 "IDF troops shot dead": Benny Morris, *Israel's Border Wars,
1949–1956: Arab Infiltration, Israeli Retaliation, and the Count-
down to the Suez War* (Oxford: Oxford University Press, 1994),
424.

42 "I still remember": Joe Sacco, *Footnotes in Gaza* (London: Jonathan
Cape, 2009), xi; Jason Burke, "What Is Palestinian Islamic Jihad
and What Is Its Relationship with Hamas," *Guardian,* Oct. 18, 2023;
"Interview—Islamic Jihad Secretary-General Ziad al-Nakhalah—
Part II" [in Arabic], Al Jazeera Arabic, Oct. 30, 2022, circa 7:15 minutes in, www.youtube.com/@aljazeera; Muhammad Shehada
(@muhammadshehad2), "In Nov 1956, #Israeli soldiers rounded
up & executed 275 Palestinians in Khan Yunis, then imposed a cur-
few on Gazans preventing retrieving the bodies," X, Nov. 24, 2022;
"Abdel Aziz al-Rantisi," Just Vision, accessed July 24, 2024, www
.justvision.org. Thanks to Muhammad Shehada for translation of
Arabic sources.

43 "recruit Hamas fighters": Gershon Baskin, "The Future of Hamas
After October 7—Part 1," *Times of Israel,* Oct. 28, 2023.

43 "responds to threat perception": Khalil Shikaki, "Willing to Com-
promise: Palestinian Public Opinion and the Peace Process," Spe-

cial Report 158, United States Institute of Peace, Jan. 2006, www
.usip.org.

43 polls showed widespread Palestinian support: Khalil Shikaki,
"Palestinians Divided," *Foreign Affairs,* Jan. 1, 2002.

44 In April 1993: Matthew Levitt, *Hamas: Politics, Charity, and Terrorism in the Service of Jihad* (New Haven, Conn.: Yale University
Press, 2006), 11–12.

44 only 18 percent: Jacob Shamir and Khalil Shikaki, *Palestinian and
Israeli Public Opinion: The Public Imperative in the Second Intifada* (Bloomington: Indiana University Press, 2010), 70.

44 "stopped the Oslo Accord": "Tricky Netanyahu: I Deceived the
US to Destroy Oslo Accords [English subtitles]," originally aired
on Channel 10 News in Israel and reposted by Palestine Diary,
Aug. 11, 2010, www.youtube.com/@abumiz.

44 new settler housing units: "Construction of New Housing Units
in 'Judea and Samaria,' 1996–2006" [in Hebrew], Israel Central
Bureau of Statistics, boardsgenerator.cbs.gov.il.

44 When Israel closed off: Amira Hass, "Israel's Closure Policy: An
Ineffective Strategy of Containment and Repression," *Journal of
Palestine Studies* 31, no. 3 (Spring 2002): 9; "Israel's Closure of the
West Bank and Gaza Strip," Human Rights Watch, July 1, 1996,
www.hrw.org.

44 more than 50 percent: Shamir and Shikaki, *Palestinian and Israeli
Public Opinion,* 72.

45 new settlement construction: "Construction of New Housing
Units in 'Judea and Samaria,' 1996–2006."

45 Barak also reneged: Gilead Sher, *The Israeli-Palestinian Peace
Negotiations, 1999–2001: Within Reach* (London: Routledge,
2006), 2.

45 generous, even reckless: Charles Enderlin, *Shattered Dreams:
The Failure of the Peace Process in the Middle East, 1995–2002,*
trans. Susan Fairfield (New York: Other Press, 2002), 250;
Jerome Slater, *Mythologies Without End: The US, Israel, and
the Arab-Israeli Conflict, 1917–2020* (Oxford: Oxford University
Press, 2021), 256; Sher, *Israeli-Palestinian Negotiations,* 107; Jer-

emy Pressman, "Visions in Collision: What Happened at Camp David and Taba?," *International Security* 28, no. 2 (2003): 5–43; Tanya Reinhardt, *Israel/Palestine: How to End the 1948 War* (New York: Seven Stories Press, 2002), 48; Yoram Meital, *Peace in Tatters: Israel, Palestine, and the Middle East* (Boulder, Colo.: Lynne Rienner Publishers, 2006), 78.

45 Palestinians would have gained: Menachem Klein, *The Jerusalem Problem: The Struggle for Permanent Status*, trans. Haim Watzman (Gainesville: University Press of Florida, 2003), 71–72; Pressman, "Visions in Collision," 18.

45 a token number: Ehud Barak, "The Myths Spread About Camp David Are Baseless," in *The Camp David Summit—What Went Wrong? Americans, Israelis, and Palestinians Analyze the Failure of the Boldest Attempt Ever to Resolve the Palestinian-Israeli Conflict*, ed. Shimon Shamir and Bruce Maddy-Weitzman (Brighton, U.K.: Sussex Academic Press, 2005), 145.

45 The Palestinian leadership: Sher, *Israeli-Palestinian Negotiations*, 95; Klein, *Jerusalem Problem*, 67.

46 After the talks failed: Joel Greenberg, "Sharon Touches a Nerve, Jerusalem Explodes," *New York Times*, Sept. 29, 2000.

46 Palestinians began throwing: Suzanne Goldenberg, "Rioting as Sharon Visits Islam Holy Site," *Guardian*, Sept. 29, 2000; Brym and Araj, "Suicide Bombing as Strategy and Interaction"; Jeremy Pressman, "The Second Intifada: Background and Causes of the Israeli-Palestinian Conflict," *Journal of Conflict Studies* 23, no. 2 (2003): 131.

46 spring of 2000: "Report of the Sharm el-Sheikh Fact-Finding Committee," United Nations: The Question of Palestine, April 30, 2000.

46 "The loss of confidence": Shikaki, "Palestinians Divided."

46 "reached a simple conclusion": Reuters and Roni Singer, "Barghouti Convicted in Deaths of Five People," *Ha'aretz*, May 20, 2004; Pressman, "Second Intifada," 128.

47 Both sides said yes: Both sides asked for clarifications and submitted written responses to Clinton. Israel's reservations in-

cluded the scope of, and timetable for, its withdrawal from the West Bank, the outlined security and military arrangements, the regime for the Temple Mount, and the fear that Israel would be required to accept even a token Palestinian right of return. Palestinian reservations included the fear that Clinton's proposal would result in a cantonized Palestinian state and a Jerusalem divided into islands, that the period proposed for Israel's withdrawal was too lengthy, that the boundaries of Israel's sovereignty over the Western Wall were unclear, and that refugees were being denied their freedom of choice to return to their homes. See Sher, *Israeli-Palestinian Negotiations,* 205–7; Slater, *Mythologies Without End,* 260–64; Yasser Abed Rabbo, "Palestinian Response to the Clinton Parameters," United States Institute of Peace, Jan. 1, 2001, www.usip.org.

47 barely more than one-third: David Makovsky, "Taba Mythchief," *National Interest,* March 1, 2003.

47 Finally, in 2005: Gideon Levy, "The Second Intifada, 20 Years On: Thousands Died in a Struggle That Failed," *Ha'aretz,* Sept. 26, 2020.

47 As the intifada: Tareq Baconi, *Hamas Contained: The Rise and Pacification of Palestinian Resistance* (Stanford, Calif.: Stanford University Press, 2018), 57.

47 Hamas violently wrested control: David Rose, "The Gaza Bombshell," *Vanity Fair,* March 3, 2008; Hass, "Israel's Closure Policy"; "PCHR Publishes 'Black Days in the Absence of Justice: Report on Bloody Fighting in the Gaza Strip from 7 to 14 June 2007,'" Palestinian Centre for Human Rights, Oct. 9, 2007, pchrgaza.org.

47 Israel, which already controlled: Hass, "Israel's Closure Policy"; Baconi, *Hamas Contained,* 106.

48 In 2007, Abbas: Ben Birnbaum, "The Visionary," *New Republic,* May 4, 2012.

48 "In deeds, Israel": Roger Cohen, "The Success That Failed," *New York Times,* Feb. 14, 2013.

48 Palestinian civil society organizations: "Open Letter: Palestinian Civil Society Call for BDS," BDS, July 9, 2005, bdsmovement.net.

48 boycotts a crime: "Israel: Anti-boycott Bill Stifles Expression," Human Rights Watch, July 13, 2011, www.hrw.org; "AJC Battles the Insidious BDS (Boycott, Divestment, Sanctions) Movement on Multiple Fronts," American Jewish Committee, accessed July 24, 2024, www.ajc.org; "US Supreme Court Lets Arkansas Law Penalising Israel Boycotts Stand," *Guardian,* Feb. 21, 2023; "Fact-Checking AIPAC's Fact Sheet on the Combating BDS Act," Foundation for Middle East Peace, Jan. 11, 2019, www.fmep.org.

48 Palestinians appealed: Peter Beaumont, "US and Israeli Intervention Led UN to Reject Palestinian Resolution," *Guardian,* Dec. 31, 2014; "Amid Middle East Violence, Security Council Fails to Adopt Competing Resolutions on Israeli Force, Hamas Role in Conflict," SC/13362, United Nations, June 1, 2018; Egypt: Draft Resolution S/2017/1060, United Nations Security Council, Dec. 18, 2017, documents.un.org; "UN Security Council Meetings & Outcomes Tables," Veto List, Dag Hammarskjöld Library, research.un.org.

48 Palestinians also urged: Anthony Blinken, "The United States Opposes the ICC Investigation into the Palestinian Situation," U.S. Department of State, March 3, 2021, www.state.gov; Times of Israel staff, "Pompeo Warns ICC of 'Consequences' for Potential War Crimes Probe of Israel," *Times of Israel,* May 16, 2020.

48 Hamas did not initiate: "What is 'The Great Return March?,'" American Friends Service Committee, www.afsc.org, April 19, 2019.

48 embraced the movement: David M. Halbfinger, "Hamas Sees Gaza Protests as Peaceful—and as a 'Deadly Weapon,'" *New York Times,* April 15, 2018.

49 As demonstrators approached: Hilo Glazer, "'42 Knees in One Day': Israeli Snipers Open Up About Shooting Gaza Protesters," *Ha'aretz,* March 6, 2020.

49 That spring, Gaza: Maha Hussaini, "Champions on Crutches: Palestinians Form First Amputee Football Team in Gaza," *Middle East Eye,* July 10, 2018.

49 "killed 223 Palestinians": "Unwilling and Unable: Israel's White-

washed Investigations of the Great March of Return Protests," B'Tselem and Palestinian Centre for Human Rights, Dec. 2021, www.btselem.org.

49 Mahmoud Abbas is: Patrick Kingsley, "Antisemitic Comments by Palestinian Leader Cause Uproar," *New York Times,* Sept. 7, 2023.

50 The settler population: "30 Years After Oslo—the Data That Shows How the Settlements Proliferated Following the Oslo Accords," Peace Now, Sept. 11, 2023, www.peacenow.org.il.

50 The UN reported: "Fact Sheet: Displacement of Palestinian Herders amid Increasing Settler Violence—September 2023," OCHA, Sept. 2023, www.unocha.org.

50 settlers had shattered: "Settler Violence Updates List," B'Tselem, accessed July 31, 2024, www.btselem.org.

51 If built without: Eric Goldstein, "Israel Settlers Rampage in Palestinian-Americans' West Bank Hometown," *Middle East Monitor,* July 27, 2023.

51 The Strip was "unlivable": Miriam Berger, "The U.N. Once Predicted Gaza Would Be 'Uninhabitable' by 2020. Two Million People Still Live There," *Washington Post,* Jan. 2, 2020.

51 Gaza's sewage plants: James McAuley and Hazem Balousha, "A Summer Day at the Beach? For Many Gazans, the Conflict Has Put an End to That, Too," *Washington Post,* Aug. 28, 2019.

51 second quarter of 2023: Palestinian Central Bureau of Statistics, Ramallah—Palestine, "Labour Force Survey: (April–June 2023) Round, (Q2/2023): Press Report Labour Force Survey," Aug. 2023.

51 The journalist Muhammad Shehada: Shehada, interview by author, May 31, 2024.

51 "an unforgivable sin": Muhammed Shehada, "When Hope Dies: Why So Many Palestinians in Gaza Are Committing Suicide," *Ha'aretz,* July 15, 2020.

51 "Palestinians have lost faith": Dana El Kurd, "Support for Violent Versus Non-violent Strategies in the Palestinian Territories," *Middle East Law and Governance* 14 (2022): 362.

52 Hamas does grow: Richard Davis, *Hamas, Popular Support, and War in the Middle East: Insurgency in the Holy Land* (Abingdon, UK: Taylor & Francis, 2016), 95, 193, 197.

52 "the orgy of occupation": Samia Nakhoul and Laila Bassam, "Who Is Mohammed Deif, the Hamas Commander Behind the Attack on Israel?," Reuters, Oct. 11, 2023.

52 "use of violence": Kirssa Cline Ryckman, "A Turn to Violence: The Escalation of Nonviolent Movements," *Journal of Conflict Resolution* 64, nos. 2–3 (2020): 319.

52 a crucial moral difference: As Gay Seidman notes, "Only a handful of ANC attacks caused civilian deaths, white or black. For the most part, ANC guerrillas limited their targets to military installations and economic sabotage, to electric pylons, military installations, power plants." See "Guerrillas in Their Midst: Armed Struggle in the South African Anti-apartheid Movement," *Mobilization: An International Quarterly* 6, no. 2 (2001): 118–19.

53 "continue preaching peace": Nelson Mandela, "I Am Prepared to Die," Nelson Mandela's statement at the opening of the defense case in the Rivonia trial, Pretoria Supreme Court, April 20, 1964.

53 "Those to whom evil": W. H. Auden, "September 1, 1939," *New Republic*, Oct. 18, 1939.

53 Shehada tells the story: Shehada, interviews by author, April 21, May 9 and 17, 2024.

3 · WAYS OF NOT SEEING

55 "a complete siege": Emanuel Fabian, "Defense Minister Announces 'Complete Siege' of Gaza: No Power, Food, or Fuel," *Times of Israel*, Oct. 9, 2023.

55 "Are you seriously": Dominick Mastrangelo, "Former Israeli PM Erupts at TV Host for Asking About Palestinian Suffering," *Hill*, Oct. 12, 2023.

55 "Me and my wife": Nicholas Kristof, "'People Are Hoping That Israel Nukes Us So We Get Rid of This Pain,'" *New York Times*, March 9, 2024.

56 "Famine is imminent": "Gaza Strip: Acute Food Insecurity Situation for 15 Feb.–15 March 2024 and Projection for 16 March–15 July 2024," IPC Analysis Portal, Integrated Food Security Phase Classification, www.ipcinfo.org.

56 "depth of the horror": Jason Burke, "Unicef Official Tells of 'Utter Annihilation' After Travelling Length of Gaza," *Guardian,* March 22, 2024.

56 "no imminent famine": Leila Fadel and Daniel Estrin, "Cease-Fire Resolution, Growing Support for Gaza in the U.S. Sour Relations with Israel," NPR, March 26, 2024.

56 "the 134 hostages": Waleed Shahid (@_waleedshahid), "MORNING JOE hosts erupt at Israel's economy minister and his government's handling of the war in Gaza," reposted from Tom Elliott (@tomselliott), X, April 4, 2024.

56 The vast majority: As of August 27, 2024, Israel had rescued 8 living hostages. Four had been released unilaterally and 105 had been released in a November 2023 deal in which Israel paused fighting and released 240 Palestinian prisoners. See Ephrat Livni, "What to Know About the Hostages Still in Gaza," *New York Times,* June 8, 2024; Elena Shao et al., "Freed Palestinians Were Mostly Young and Not Convicted of Crimes," *New York Times,* Dec. 1, 2023, updated Dec. 2, 2023; *Times of Israel* staff, "Rescued Hostage Said Kept in Total Darkness During Captivity, Showered Once a Month," *Times of Israel,* Aug. 29, 2024.

56 several former hostages: Nir Gontarz, "Rescued Israeli Hostage: 'Our Greatest Fear Was Israeli Planes,'" *Ha'aretz,* June 9, 2024; Itamar Eichner and Yael Ciechanover, "Hostage Families Have Tense Meeting with War Cabinet, Say Netanyahu 'Detached' from Their Concerns," Ynet News, Dec. 5, 2023; Ran Shimoni, "They Were Held Captive by Hamas, but Their Biggest Fear Was Israeli Airstrikes," *Ha'aretz,* Dec. 11, 2023.

56 seeing Israelis protesting: Noga Tarnopolsky (@_NTarnopolsky), "Andrey Kozlov, rescued from Hamas captivity one week ago, in new statement: 'Almost every Saturday, they showed us the rallies that took place in Tel Aviv,'" X, June 15, 2024.

57   "people's eyes glaze over": Omer Bartov, "As a Former IDF Soldier and Historian of Genocide, I Was Deeply Disturbed by My Recent Visit to Israel," *Guardian,* Aug. 13, 2024.

57   "all Jews are responsible": Babylonian Talmud, Shevuot 39a.

57   one "person will not say": Babylonian Talmud, Sanhedrin 37a.

58   "The 'Gaza Health Ministry'": "Israel Works to Protect Civilians; Hamas Uses Them as Human Shields," AIPAC memo, Nov. 9, 2023.

58   clearly untrue: Bari Weiss, "Iran Attacked Israel. What Comes Next?," *Honestly with Bari Weiss,* podcast, April 16, 2024, circa 33:30 minutes in.

58   For this reason: Glenn Kessler, "Biden's Dismissal of the Reported Palestinian Death Toll," *Washington Post,* Nov. 1, 2023.

58   first five weeks: Nancy A. Youssef, "U.S. Officials Have Growing Confidence in Death Toll Reports from Gaza," *Wall Street Journal,* Nov. 11, 2023; Gabrielle Tétrault-Farber, "Despite Biden's Doubts, Humanitarian Agencies Consider Gaza Toll Reliable," Reuters, Oct. 27, 2023.

59   numbers were too low: "One Name, Two Lists: Matching Open Source Evidence with Official Gaza Death Tolls," Airwars, July 24, 2024, gaza-civilians.airwars.org.

59   the Health Ministry said: "Gaza Conflict: Thousands Remain Unidentified as Death Toll Reaches 40,000," Ben van der Merwe, Josephine Franks, and Aisling Ní Chúláin, Sky News, Aug. 15, 2024; Michael Spagat, "Tracking Gaza's War Death Toll: Ministry of Health Improves Accuracy in Latest Report," Action on Armed Violence, Sept. 24, 2024.

59   almost thirty-five thousand: "Hostilities in the Gaza Strip and Israel—Reported Impact | Day 215," United Nations Office for the Coordination of Humanitarian Affairs, May 8, 2024, www .ochaopt.org.

59   Netanyahu put the number: CBS/AFP staff, "Israel's Netanyahu Says Militants Make Up About Half of Gaza Deaths," CBS News, May 14, 2024.

59   the Israeli journalist: Yuval Abraham (@yuval_abraham), "Israeli

intelligence secretly surveilled officials in Gaza's Health Ministry to check if their data on the number of civilians killed in Gaza is 'reliable' . . . ," X, Jan. 24, 2024.

59 68 percent: Zeina Jamaluddine, Francesco Checchi, and Oona M. R. Campbell, "Excess Mortality in Gaza: Oct. 7–26, 2023," *Lancet,* Dec. 9, 2023, first published Nov. 26, 2023.

60 more than 70 percent: "Emergency Report for the Health Sector, Day (169) of the Aggression, Saturday, March 23, 2024" [in Arabic], Palestinian Ministry of Health/Gaza (t.me/MOHMedia Gaza), March 25, 2024. The ministry moved away from reporting 72 percent women and children in its PDFs as of March 29, 2024. See "Emergency Report for the Health Sector, Day (173) of the Aggression, Wednesday, March 27, 2024" [in Arabic], Palestinian Ministry of Health/Gaza (t.me/MOHMediaGaza), March 29, 2024.

60 around 60 percent: Professor Mike Spagat, "Gaza Ministry of Health Releases Detailed New Casualty Data Amidst Confusion of UN's Death Numbers in Gaza," Action on Armed Violence, May 28, 2024, and an interview with Professor Spagat in early June 2024 to clarify the number of elderly killed that the Ministry of Health had managed to identify as of April 30, 2024.

60 had killed were "terrorists": "Dr. Phil's Exclusive Interview with Prime Minister Benjamin Netanyahu," *Dr. Phil Primetime,* May 10, 2024, circa 26:30 minutes in, www.youtube.com /@DrPhilPrimetime.

60 "It's a bit rich": Allan Woods, "The Death Toll in Gaza Is Enormous. A Sudden Shift in UN Numbers Reveals the True Count Is Another Source of Conflict," *Toronto Star,* May 16, 2024.

60 80 percent of reported fatalities: Eleven thousand three hundred and fifty-five is only the number of children the Health Ministry had managed to identify as of August 31, 2024, whose names were released in a list published on September 16, 2024. See Palestinian Ministry of Health/Gaza (t.me/MOHMediaGaza), "Martyrs as of 31-08-2024" [in Arabic], Telegram, Sept. 16, 2024. See also Spagat, "Tracking Gaza's War Death Toll."

60 11,350 children: On the ministry's totals only including trauma deaths, see "Dr. Ola Awad, President of the Palestinian Central Bureau of Statistics, Speaks to AOAV About Casualty Counting and the Death Figures Coming from Gaza," Action on Armed Violence, Nov. 20, 2023. The ministry is reportedly expected to release a total of all deaths it has managed to account for, including so-called indirect deaths, at the end of 2024. The above paragraphs on the Ministry's reporting are indebted to the guidance provided by Professor Michael Spagat and Ben van der Merwe in multiple interviews between June and August 2024.

60 thirty-four Palestinian children: The first Israeli airstrikes on Gaza were launched on October 7. See Ghousoon Bisharat, "A Palestinian Physician in Israel Wrestles with Her Duty in the War," *+972 Magazine*, Nov. 16, 2023. There were 330 days between October 7, 2023, and the Health Ministry's most recent list of fatalities as of the time of writing, reflecting deaths identified by August 31, 2024.

61 "Hamas is responsible": AIPAC (@AIPAC), "Palestinians in Gaza are nothing more than human shields for Hamas. Blocking them from evacuating. Using them as pawns to fuel their propaganda machine," X, Oct. 14, 2023.

61 In lobbying materials: AIPAC, "14.3 Billion for Israel's Security," May 6, 2024, www.aipac.org; AIPAC, "Israel Takes Additional Steps to Improve the Humanitarian Situation in Gaza," April 11, 2024, aipacorg.app.box.com; AIPAC, "Israel Facilitates Humanitarian Aid to Gaza as Hamas Continues to Attack," March 20, 2024, aipacorg.app.box.com; AIPAC, "Israel's Multi-front Threats," March 13, 2024, aipacorg.app.box.com; AIPAC, "October 7th Factsheet," Nov. 28, 2023, aipacorg.app.box.com; AIPAC, "Frequently Asked Questions: Israel at War," Nov. 22, 2023, www.aipac.org; AIPAC, "Israel Works to Protect Palestinian Civilians; Hamas Uses Them as Human Shields," Nov. 9, 2023, aipacorg.app.box.com.

61 It doesn't mean fighting: In the words of the Yale international law professor Aslı Ü. Bâli, "The definition of using human shields

for a matter of international law is the deliberate placement of civilians in proximity to military objectives during a conflict. It is not the presence of civilians in densely populated areas from which armed groups also operate." Ezra Klein, "The Disastrous Relationship Between Israel, Palestinians, and the U.N.," *The Ezra Klein Show,* podcast, May 17, 2024, circa 45 minutes in.

61 "From the American Revolution": Neve Gordon, "On Human Shields," *London Review of Books,* Dec. 1, 2023.

61 Twenty-four schools: There are twelve primary and twelve high schools, as well as nineteen kindergartens, within a 1.5-kilometer radius of the IDF's General Staff building and the Israeli Defense Ministry. See "Tel Aviv Municipality Geographical Information System," accessed June 10, 2024, gisn.tel-aviv.gov.il. See also Nir Mann, "Does the Presence of the IDF's HQ in Tel Aviv Endanger the City's Population?," *Ha'aretz,* June 9, 2012.

62 "their legal obligations": "Article 51—Protection of the Civilian Population," in "Protocol Additional to the Geneva Conventions of 12 August 1949, and Relating to the Protection of Victims of International Armed Conflicts (Protocol 1)," June 8, 1977, ihl-databases.icrc.org.

62 "released all the restraints": Emmanuel Fabian and Jacob Magid, "Gallant: Israel Moving to Full Offense, Gaza Will Never Go Back to What It Once Was," *Times of Israel,* Oct. 10, 2023; Yagil Levy, "The Israeli Army Has Dropped the Restraint in Gaza, and the Data Shows Unprecedented Killing," *Ha'aretz,* Dec. 9, 2023.

62 a thousand "power targets": Yuval Abraham, "'A Mass Assassination Factory': Inside Israel's Calculated Bombing of Gaza," *+972 Magazine,* Nov. 30, 2023.

62 "Remember that the citizens": Alan Dershowitz (@AlanDersh), "The Citizens of Gaza Are Supporters of Hamas. #law #lawyer #news #trending #trump #biden #shorts," X, Nov. 2, 2023.

63 "Hamas overwhelmingly represents": Morton A. Klein, "Palestinian Arabs Overwhelmingly Support Hamas & Their Genocidal Aspirations—ZOA's Mort Klein Op-Ed in the Federalist," Zionist Organization of America, Oct. 25, 2023, www.zoa.org.

63 didn't win a majority: "The Second 2006 PLC Elections: Lists Voter per Districts," Central Elections Commission Palestine, accessed July 24, 2024, www.elections.ps.

63 By some accounts: "The Palestinian Legislative Council Elections of January 25th, 2006: Results, Delegates, Formation of Government," Office of the Konrad Adenauer Foundation to the Palestinian Autonomous Territories, Ramallah, April 2006, www.kas.de.

63 more than 60 percent: Khalil Shikaki, "The Polls: What the Palestinians Really Voted For," *Newsweek International,* Feb. 6, 2006.

63 polls conducted in Gaza: Amaney Jamal and Michael Robbins, "What Palestinians Really Think of Hamas," *Foreign Affairs,* Oct. 25, 2023.

63 about one-quarter: In January 2023, anyone who would have been eligible to vote in the January 2006 elections (seventeen years previous) would be at least thirty-five. The U.S. Census Bureau statistics for Gaza for January 2023 estimate a total population of 2,098,389 and a population of thirty-five and above of 465,131, or 22.2 percent of the total. (Note that the 2023 numbers are based on projections and refer to the month of January. Since the Palestinian legislative elections were held at the end of the month, it is possible that there would be a small number of people who would have been eighteen during the elections but listed as being thirty-four years old, but taking these individuals into account would not substantially change the results, especially since some portion of the population above thirty-five also died between January and October.) U.S. Census Bureau, International Database, Gaza Strip; generated by Aron Wander using census.gov/data-tools; "Voters According to Age Groups," 2006 PLC Elections Statistics, Central Elections Commission—Palestine, accessed July 30, 2024, www.elections.ps.

64 "In any combat situation": Amna Nawaz, "Netanyahu Adviser on Hostages and Risks of Continued Bombing," *PBS News Hour,* Oct. 24, 2023, circa 5:55 minutes in, www.pbs.org.

64 "You didn't tell": "Israeli PM Netanyahu Speaks Amid Expanding Ground Operation; Police Visited Maine Gunman's Home Weeks Before Shootings," *CNN News Central,* Oct. 30, 2023, transcripts .cnn.com.

64 In the first month: Michael Crowley and Edward Wong, "Under Scrutiny over Gaza, Israel Points to Civilian Toll of U.S. Wars," *New York Times,* Nov. 7, 2023.

64 Mexicans can import soap: Farah Najjar and Hosam Salem, "From Wedding Dresses to Soap: Gaza Event Highlights Israeli Siege," Al Jazeera, Aug. 2, 2018; "Collective Punishment: A New Ban on the Marketing of Furniture from Gaza" [in Hebrew], Gisha, June 4, 2023.

65 Israel exercises that control: Even before October 7, Israel controlled Gaza's population registry, which gave it control over who could legally enter and exit. See "One-Way Ticket," Gisha, Dec. 25, 2022, www.gisha.org.

65 "This business of destroying": *Times of Israel* staff, "IDF Spokesman Says Hamas Can't Be Destroyed, Drawing Retort from PM: 'That's War's Goal,'" *Times of Israel,* June 20, 2024; Nadeen Ebrahim, "Israel's Return to Areas of Gaza It Said Were Clear of Hamas Raises Doubts About Its Military Strategy," CNN, May 13, 2024.

66 In July 2024: Jacob Magid, "Knesset Vote Overwhelmingly Against Palestinian Statehood, Days Before PM's US Trip," *Times of Israel,* July 18, 2024.

66 Israel still imprisons Marwan: Ha'aretz Staff, "Marwan Barghouti Vows to 'Honor Mandela's Struggle,'" *Ha'aretz,* December 10, 2013.

67 In 2008, Hamas's: Samia Nakhoul, "How Hamas Secretly Built a 'Mini-Army to Fight Israel," Reuters, Oct. 16, 2023; Sarah El Deeb, "What Is Hamas? The Group That Rules the Gaza Strip Has Fought Several Rounds of War with Israel," Associated Press, Oct. 15, 2023; Madjid Zerrouky, "Hamas's Relentless Efforts to Build Up Its Military Arsenal in Gaza," *Le Monde,* Oct. 11, 2023;

Ari Flanzraich, "Israel Says It Intercepted a Hamas Long-Range Missile with New Defense System," *Wall Street Journal,* live coverage feed, Nov. 5, 2023; Nagham Zbeedat, " 'Return of Martyrdom': 'The Engineer' Yahya Ayyash Trends as Hamas Threatens More Suicide Attacks," *Ha'aretz,* Aug. 20, 2024.

67 some close observers: Tareq Baconi, "What Was Hamas Thinking?," *Foreign Policy,* Nov. 22, 2023.

67 Hamas has seen: "Public Opinion Poll No (89)," Palestinian Center for Policy and Survey Research, Sept. 13, 2023, www.pcpsr.org; "Public Opinion Poll No (92)," Palestinian Center for Policy and Survey Research, July 10, 2024, www.pcpsr.org.

68 "If we continue": Ami Ayalon with Anthony David, *Friendly Fire: How Israel Became Its Own Worst Enemy and the Hope for Its Future* (Lebanon, NH: Steerforth Press, 2020), 251.

68 "Whenever I open": Susannah Heschel, introduction to *Essential Writings,* by Abraham Joshua Heschel, ed. Susannah Heschel (Maryknoll, N.Y.: Orbis Books, 2011), 17.

69 "God's voice is shaking": Edward K. Kaplan, *Spiritual Radical: Abraham Joshua Heschel in America, 1940–1972* (New Haven, Conn.: Yale University Press, 2007), 321.

69 "It is weird": Abraham Joshua Heschel, "The Moral Outrage of Vietnam," *Fellowship,* Sept. 1966, cited in Kaplan, *Spiritual Radical.*

69 "Who said that": France 24/AFP staff, "Assad Denies Ordering Brutal Syrian Crackdown," France 24, Dec. 7, 2011, updated Dec. 8, 2011.

70 "need to be careful": Kareem Fahim, "Saudis Face Mounting Pressure over Civilian Deaths in Yemen Conflict," *New York Times,* Sept. 29, 2015.

70 claims as "propaganda": Chris Woods, "Does the U.S. Ignore Its Civilian Casualties in Iraq and Syria?," *New York Times,* Aug. 17, 2016.

70 "civilians as human shields": Arab News staff, "Coalition's Priority Is to Protect Civilians," *Arab News,* Feb. 14, 2017.

70 "uses the residents": Neve Gordon and Nicola Perugini, "Why We Need to Challenge Russia's Human Shields Narrative," Al Jazeera, April 3, 2022.

70 "use defenseless women": Neve Gordon and Nicola Perugini, *Human Shields: A History of People in the Line of Fire* (Oakland: University of California Press, 2020), chap. 9, epub.

70 a vast labyrinth: See, for example, Tom Mangold and John Penycate, *The Tunnels of Cu Chi* (New York: Random House, 1985).

71 the American Jewish Committee: "AJC Deeply Regrets ICC Over-reach in Palestinian Case," American Jewish Committee, Feb. 5, 2021, www.ajc.org.

71 "genocide of the Uyghur": "Jonathan Greenblatt Remarks to Students at Brown University," Anti-Defamation League, Feb. 22, 2024, www.adl.org.

71 While some Jews: The Israeli writer Yossi Klein Halevi describes "a growing contempt in parts of the [Israeli religious Zionist] community for Western values and humanistic values, as if those who are antithetical to Jewish values [sic]." See Donniel Hartman and Yossi Klein Halevi, "Israel at War—the Paradox of Religious Zionism," *For Heaven's Sake,* podcast, circa 20:30 minutes in.

71 they should target Iran: "Dr. Phil's Exclusive Interview with Prime Minister Benjamin Netanyahu," Dr. Phil Primetime, circa 41:10 minutes in, www.youtube.com/@DrPhilPrimetime.

71 "at a moral disconnect": Yossi Klein Halevi, "The Lonely People of History," *Times of Israel,* Nov. 12, 2023.

72 "Many of the dead": Isabel Kershner, "Facing Global Outrage, Netanyahu Calls Civilian Deaths in Rafah Strike 'Tragic Accident,'" *New York Times,* May 27, 2024.

72 "One thousand prosecutors": "PM MK Netanyahu in 40-Signature Debate: If We Give In, the Murder and Rape Will Recur, We Won't Bring Back the Hostages, and We'll Give a Great Victory to Terrorism," Knesset News, May 27, 2024, main.knesset.gov.il.

72 "The greatness of this people": "'Eichmann in Jerusalem': An Exchange of Letters Between Gershom Scholem and Hannah

Arendt," in Hannah Arendt, *The Jew as Pariah: Jewish Identity and Politics in the Modern Age,* ed. Ron H. Feldman (New York: Grove Press, 1978), 247.

73 "raise your eyes toward": Ezekiel 33:25–26.

4 · THE NEW NEW ANTISEMITISM

75 Between October 7, 2023: Tweets were extracted from keyword searches using the Meltwater platform.

76 The British scholar David Feldman: Isaac Chotiner, "Where Does Antisemitism Come From?," *New Yorker,* Nov. 7, 2023.

76 Donald Trump's closing advertisement: Trump's ad also featured images of Janet Yellen, the Jewish chair of the Federal Reserve, and the Jewish investor and philanthropist George Soros, a frequent target of antisemitic conspiracy theories. See Josh Marshall, "Trump Rolls Out Anti-Semitic Closing Ad," *Talking Points Memo,* November 5, 2016.

76 A Pittsburgh man obsessed: Yonat Shimron and Jack Jenkins, "Pittsburgh Suspect's Hatred of Jews, HIAS Part of Larger Anti-Immigrant Surge," *Religion News Service,* Oct. 29, 2018.

76 after protesters in Venezuela: Philissa Cramer, "Venezuela's Maduro Blames 'International Zionism' for Unrest After Disputed Vote," *Times of Israel,* Aug. 8, 2024; Yashar Ali (@yashar), "Zionism can barely secure one country the size of New Jersey but somehow has the power to control the world and impact elections in nearly . . . ," X, Aug. 4, 2024.

76 violent anti-immigrant riots: David Miller (@Tracking_Power), "The 'State of Israel' is burning down the UK. As I have been saying, 'Tommy Robinson' is a Zionist asset. Here he is admitting that the . . . ," X, Aug. 4, 2024.

77 first two decades: Geoffrey Levin, *Our Palestine Question: Israel and American Jewish Dissent, 1948–1978* (New Haven, Conn.: Yale University Press, 2023), 14–16. See also chaps. 1 and 2.

77 "common psychological roots": Peter Novick, *The Holocaust in American Life* (Boston: Houghton Mifflin, 1999), 116.

79 American Jewish groups raised: Naomi Cohen, *American Jews and the Zionist Idea* (New York: Ktav, 1975), 138–39, quoted in Chaim Waxman, "American Jewish Identity and New Patterns of Philanthropy," in *The Call of the Homeland: Diaspora Nationalisms, Past and Present,* ed. Allon Gal, Athena Leoussi, and Anthony Smith (Leiden, NL: Brill, 2010), 88.

79 After the war: Lawrence Grossman, "Transformation Through Crisis: The American Jewish Committee and the Six-Day War," *American Jewish History* 86, no. 1 (March 1998): 52.

79 "The Six-Day War": Steven T. Rosenthal, *Irreconcilable Differences? The Waning of the American Jewish Love Affair with Israel* (Waltham, Mass.: Brandeis University Press, 2001), xiii.

79 Black activist groups: Robin D. G. Kelly, "Yes, I Said 'National Liberation,'" *Counterpunch,* Feb. 24, 2016; Roy Dahlberg, "Suggested Middle East Resolution, Re: Arab-Israeli Reaction and Implications, NIC Resolution," *New Left Notes* 2, no. 24 (June 19, 1967). In the SDS database, the date for the issue in which Dahlberg's piece appears is mistakenly listed as June 29.

79 "zionism [*sic*] and Israeli imperialism": United Nations General Assembly, "Situation in South Africa Resulting from the Policies of Apartheid," Resolution A/RES/3151(XXVIII), Dec. 14, 1973, United Nations Digital Library, digitallibrary.un.org.

79 In 1974, Arnold Forster: Before Forster and Epstein coined the term "new antisemitism" in the United States, writers in France and Israel toyed with similar notions. The Holocaust survivor Jacques Givet used the term "neo-antisemitism" in his 1968 book about the left and Israel and the historian Léon Poliakov published *From Anti-Zionism to Antisemitism* in 1969. Reflecting on similar developments in Israel, the British philosopher Brian Klug questions whether Yehoshofat Harkabi's writings in the mid-1960s constitute the origins of the "new antisemitism" discourse but argues that its premise can be traced to early Zionist texts such as Herzl's. See Jacques Givet, *La gauche contre Israël? Essai sur le néo-antisémitisme* [The Left Against Israel? Essay on Neo-Antisemitism] (Paris: J.J. Pauvert, 1988); Léon Poliakov,

De l'antisionisme à l'antisémitisme [From Anti-Zionism to Anti-semitism] (Paris: Calmann-Levy, 1969); Brian Klug, "Interrogating 'New Anti-Semitism,'" *Ethnic and Racial Studies* 36, no. 3 (2012), 468–70.

80 "the Radical Left": Arnold Forster and Benjamin Epstein, *The New Anti-Semitism* (New York: McGraw-Hill, 1974), 7.

80 Leftists sometimes make Jews: The Marxist academic Moishe Postone has argued that antisemitism has "a pseudo-emancipatory dimension that other forms of racism rarely have," sometimes serving as "a primitive critique . . . of capitalist modernity." It can mask itself as "the expression of a movement of the little people" against "Jews," who are seen as "constituting an immensely powerful, abstract, intangible global form of power that dominates the world." See Moishe Postone, "History and Helplessness: Mass Mobilization and Contemporary Forms of Anticapitalism," *Public Culture* 18, no. 1 (2006), 99; Moishe Postone, "Zionism, Anti-semitism and the Left," interview by Martin Thomas, *Solidarity* 3, no. 166 (2010).

80 The 1960s and 1970s: Jonathan Judaken, *Critical Theories of Anti-Semitism* (New York: Columbia University Press, 2024), 228–9.

80 When Czechs launched: Zuzana Poláčková and Pieter C. van Duin, "Anti-Zionism and the Fight Against Anti-Semitism in Czechoslovakia, 1967–1969," *Historický Časopis* [Historical Journal] 68, no. 5, (2020): 881.

80 "Zionist controlled press": Student Nonviolent Coordinating Committee, "Third World Round Up—Test Your Knowledge: The Palestine Problem," *SNCC Newsletter,* June–July 1967, 5.

81 it usually coincides with: Adam Haber and Matylda Figlerowicz, "Anatomy of a Moral Panic," *Jewish Currents,* May 2, 2024.

81 American progressives: "Republicans and Democrats Grow Even Further Apart in Views of Israel, Palestinians," Pew Research Center, Jan. 23, 2018, www.pewresearch.org; Lydia Saad, "Young Adults' Views on Middle East Changing Most," *Gallup News,* March 24, 2023.

81 "epitomize the Radical Left": Jonathan Greenblatt, "Remarks by

Jonathan Greenblatt to the ADL Virtual National Leadership Summit," Anti-Defamation League, May 1, 2022, www.adl.org.

82 "more common on the right": Eitan Hersh and Laura Royden, "Antisemitic Attitudes Across the Ideological Spectrum," *Political Research Quarterly* 76, no. 2 (June 2023): 698.

82 "Even when primed": Ibid., 708.

82 Americans who supported punishing: Ibid.

83 Republicans who opposed: Michael Tesler, "The Perils of Conflating Anti-Zionism with Antisemitism," *Good Authority*, June 5, 2024; "Nationscape," Voter Study Group, accessed July 30, 2024, www.voterstudygroup.org.

83 A 2018 study: Jeffrey Cohen, "Left, Right, and Antisemitism in European Public Opinion," *Politics and Religion Journal* 12, no. 2 (2018): 361–62.

83 A 2021 study: András Kovács and György Fischer, "Antisemitic Prejudices in Europe: Survey in 16 European Countries," Action and Protection League of Europe, Budapest, 2021, 1:82, 95.

83 right-wing antipathy: Ben Lorber, "The Right's Anti-Israel Insurgents," *Jewish Currents*, May 15, 2024.

83 The Hersh and Royden study: Hersh and Royden, "Antisemitic Attitudes," 704.

84 Three separate studies: Dirk Jacobs et al., "The Impact of the Conflict in Gaza on Antisemitism in Belgium," *Patterns of Prejudice* 45, no. 4 (2011): 341–60; Matteo Vergani et al., "When and How Does Anti-Semitism Occur? The Different Trigger Mechanisms Associated with Different Types of Criminal and Non-criminal Hate Incidents," *Deviant Behavior* 43, no. 9 (2021): 1135–52; Ayal Feinberg, "Homeland Violence and Diaspora Insecurity: An Analysis of Israel and American Jewry," *Politics and Religion* 13, no. 1 (2020): 1–27.

84 Nearly four months: Josh Campbell, "Picture: FBI on Alert for Threats to the Jewish Community Ahead of Passover, Director Says," CNN, April 18, 2024.

85 German Americans were: Robert Siegel, "Lynching of Robert

Prager Underlined Anti-German Sentiment During World War I," NPR, April 6, 2017.

85 while some Americans: After October 7, hate crimes against Arabs and Muslims spiked in New York and Los Angeles. A six-year-old Palestinian boy was murdered in Chicago, a Palestinian man was stabbed in Texas, and three Palestinian students were shot in Vermont. See Russell Contreras, "Anti-Arab and Antisemitic Hate Crimes Surging in NYC, LA," Axios, Oct. 31, 2023; Eric Levenson, Whitney Wild, and Bill Kirkos, "Landlord Accused of Killing 6-Year-Old Palestinian American Boy Pleads Not Guilty to Murder and Hate Crime Charges," CNN, Oct. 30, 2023; Max Matza, "Stabbing of US Palestinian a Hate Crime—Texas Police," BBC, Feb. 8, 2024; Tom Llamas and Mirna Alsharif, "Palestinian Students Shot in Vermont Say the Suspect Waited for and Targeted Them," NBC News, Jan. 17, 2024.

85 Hersh and Royden discovered: Laura Royden and Eitan Hersh, "The Young American Left and Attitudes About Israel," June 9, 2021, 5–6, www.eitanhersh.com.

86 "Zionism is fundamental": Charles Blow, "The Question of Anti-Zionism and Antisemitism," *New York Times,* Nov. 15, 2023.

86 "the central role Israel": Fox News, "WATCH LIVE: Columbia University President Testifies Before House Panel on Campus Antisemitism," Facebook, April 17, 2024, circa 1:11:38 minutes in, www.facebook.com/FoxNews.

87 "Fuck the Jews": "Audit of Antisemitic Incidents 2023," Anti-Defamation League, April 16, 2024, www.adl.org.

87 "river to the sea": Ibid.; Shane Burley and Jonah ben Avraham, "Examining the ADL's Antisemitism Audit," *Jewish Currents,* June 17, 2024; "Slogan: 'From the River to the Sea Palestine Will Be Free,'" Anti-Defamation League, Oct. 26, 2023, www.adl.org.

87 Israel's foreign minister: Israel Katz (@Israel_katz), ".@sanchez castejon, your deputy @Yolanda_Diaz_ is calling for the establishment of a Palestinian state from the river to the sea. If you do not fire her immediately," X, June 1, 2024.

87   maintain that the slogan: Yousef Munayyer, "What Does 'From
the River to the Sea' Really Mean?," *Jewish Currents,* June 11, 2021;
Maha Nassar, "'From the River to the Sea, Palestine Will Be
Free,'" *Rethinking Palestine,* Nov. 30, 2023.

87   "democratic state in Palestine": Mohammed Rashid, "Towards
a Democratic State in Palestine," *Palestine Essays,* no. 24, Palestine Liberation Organization Research Center, Nov. 1970, 39.

87   Congresswoman Rashida Tlaib: Ben Sales, "'From the River
to the Sea': The Slogan That Led to Rashida Tlaib's Censure,
Explained," *Times of Israel,* Nov. 8, 2023.

88   University of Chicago poll: Robert Pape, "Understanding Campus Fears After October 7 and How to Reduce Them," University
of Chicago and Chicago Project on Security and Threats, March
2024, ii.

88   use similar expressions: See, for example, Rachel Fink, "Netanyahu Minister to Nations Recognizing Palestine: 'Only Israel
from the River to the Sea,'" *Ha'aretz,* May 22, 2024. In January
of that year, Netanyahu stated, "With an accord or without an
accord, Israel must have security control over the entire territory
West of the Jordan River." See Reuters Staff, "Israel Says Its Gaza
Plans Clash with 'Palestinian Sovereignty,'" Reuters, Jan. 20,
2024.

88   The founding charter: "Likud Party: Original Party Platform
(1977)," Jewish Virtual Library, accessed July 28, 2024, www
.jewishvirtuallibrary.org.

88   several hundred thousand more: Morris, *Righteous Victims,* 327.

88   accused of genocide: "Genocide in Gaza: Analysis of Interna-
tional Law and Its Application to Israel's Military Actions Since
October 7, 2023," University Network for Human Rights, Boston
University School of Law International Human Rights Clinic,
Cornell Law School International Human Rights Clinic, Uni-
versity of Pretoria Centre for Human Rights, Yale Law School
Lowenstein Human Rights Project, May 15, 2024.

89   In its catalog: Burley and ben Avraham, "Examining the ADL's

Antisemitism Audit"; "ADL H.E.A.T. Map," Anti-Defamation League, accessed July 31, 2024, www.adl.org.

89 Even if armed: Under international law, Israelis in illegal settlements in the West Bank are considered civilians unless they engage in military operations. See "Use of Force in the Occupied West Bank," Human Rights Watch, May 8, 2024, www.hrw.org.

89 Arabic newspapers used: Juan Cole, "'Intifada' in Arabic Just Means Uprising or Mass Protest; It Is Used for the Jewish Warsaw Uprising," *Informed Comment,* May 1, 2024.

90 the acid test: For instance, asked in a March 2022 interview with *The New Yorker* whether "anti-Semitism is something that Jews themselves get to define," Jonathan Greenblatt replied, "The people from different marginalized groups who've been struggling with that marginalization for some time have the right to say what feels right and what doesn't feel right." See Isaac Chotiner, "Is Anti-Zionism Anti-Semitism?," *New Yorker,* May 11, 2022.

91 "antisemitic mobs have taken": Benjamin Netanyahu (@netanyahu), X, April 24, 2024. The tweet includes a video of Netanyahu.

91 A May 2024 study: "Majority of Jewish College Students Say They Feel Less Safe due to Encampments; 61% Report Antisemitism During Campus Protests," Hillel International, May 13, 2024, www.hillel.org; "Hillel International: Survey of Jewish and Non-Jewish College Students," Benson Strategy Group, May 9, 2024.

91 At Cornell: Daniel Arkin, Tom Winter, and Dennis Romero, "Cornell University Student Threatened to Stab and Rape Jewish Students and 'Shoot Up' School, Prosecutors Say," NBC News, Oct. 31, 2023.

91 At the University of Georgia: "Audit of Antisemitic Incidents 2023," Anti-Defamation League.

91 asked if they were Jewish: WSYX staff, "DeWine Orders Increased Police Patrols at OSU Following Anti-Semitic Hate Crime," WSYX, Nov. 10, 2023.

92 "A sizeable minority": Eitan Hersh, "The Complicated Rela-

tionship Between Ideology and Attitudes About Jews and Israel," prepared for the Jim Joseph Foundation, Feb. 2024, 5, jimjosephfoundation.org.

92 "all Israeli civilians": Ibid., 4.

92 "campus anger today": Pape, "Understanding Campus Fears After October 7 and How to Reduce Them," 16.

93 most vocal Zionist activists: Noah Bernstein and Rebecca Massel, "'The Jewish Community Is Alone': Columbia SSI President Speaks at Congressional Roundtable," *Columbia Spectator,* March 1, 2024; Sahar Tartak, "I Was Stabbed in the Eye at Yale," *Free Press,* July 30, 2024.

93 "Instead of understanding": Daniel Randall, *Confronting Antisemitism on the Left: Arguments for Socialists* (London: No Pasaran Media, 2021), chap. 2, Kindle.

94 weeks and months after: Esha Karam "'Doxxing Truck' Displaying Names and Faces of Affiliates It Calls 'Antisemites' Comes to Columbia," *Columbia Spectator,* Oct. 25, 2023; Rachel Moon and Jennifer Igbonoba, "'Doxing Truck' Displays Names, Faces of Pro-Palestinian Students, Draws Ire from Officials," *GW Hatchet,* Nov. 30, 2023; Shanon Thaler, "'Doxxing Trucks' Expand to Columbia, UPenn to Expose Campuses' 'Leading Antisemites,'" *New York Post,* Oct. 26, 2023; Joyce Kim and Asher Montgomery, "Doxxed Harvard Students Decry 'Heinous and Aggressive' Online Harassment, Call for Greater Support from University," *Harvard Crimson,* Dec. 8, 2023; Nicky Andrew, "'Doxxing Truck' Displays Names and Images of CU Boulder Ethnic Studies Faculty on Campus," *Denver Post,* Jan. 31, 2024; Esma Okutan and Tristan Hernandez, "'Doxxing Truck' Appears on Yale's Campus, Displays Student Names and Photos," *Yale Daily News,* Nov. 17, 2023; Middle East Eye staff, "Republican Donors Funded Doxxing Campaign Against Pro-Palestinian University Students," *Middle East Eye,* May 14, 2024.

94 In several instances: Shannon Thaler, "Harvard 'Doxxing Truck' Parks Outside Homes of Students Who Blamed Israel for Hamas Attacks," *New York Post,* Oct. 26, 2023.

94 Numerous pro-Palestinian students: Kim and Montgomery, "Doxxed Harvard Students Decry 'Heinous and Aggressive' Online Harassment"; David Thomas, "Pro-Palestine Lawyer Sues Law Firm Foley over Rescinded Job Offer," Reuters, May 30, 2024; Karen Sloan, "Anti-Israel Comments Prompt Winston & Strawn to Rescind NYU Law Student's Job Offer," Reuters, Oct. 11, 2023; Karen Sloan, "Law Firm Davis Polk Revokes Job Offers to Harvard, Columbia Students over Israel Statements," Reuters, Oct. 18, 2023.

94 A May 2024 study: Bianca Ho and Kieran Doyle, "US Student Pro-Palestine Demonstrations Remain Overwhelmingly Peaceful," ACLED Brief, Armed Conflict Location & Event Data Project, May 10, 2024, acleddata.com

94 Pro-Palestinian protesters: Maryam Alwan, "(Pro-)Palestinian Lives Do Not Matter to Columbia University," *Columbia Spectator,* Feb. 1, 2024; Neil Bedi et al., "How Counterprotesters at U.C.L.A. Provoked Violence, Unchecked for Hours," *New York Times,* May 3, 2024; Surina Venkat, "Motorist Charged with Assault for Striking CUAD Protester with Car at Picket Outside Trustee's Home," *Columbia Spectator,* May 8, 2024.

95 In April, police: Maura Zurick, "65-Year-Old Man 'Lucky to Be Alive' After Arrest at Campus Protest," *Newsweek,* April 30, 2024.

95 In May, they gassed: "After Police Remove Tents, Make Arrests, Protesters at UW-Madison Rebuild Encampment," *WPR,* May 1, 2024.

95 At Dartmouth, police: Vimal Patel, "Police Treatment of a Dartmouth Professor Stirs Anger and Debate," *New York Times,* May 3, 2024.

95 Columbia suspended its chapter: Sarah Huddleston and Chris Mendel, "Columbia Suspends SJP and JVP Following 'Unauthorized' Thursday Walkout," *Columbia Spectator,* updated Nov. 11, 2023.

95 "protect Jewish students": Anti-Defamation League (@ADL), "Finally. Thank you, @Columbia, for enforcing your policies & acting in a way consistent with your legal & moral obligations

to protect Jewish students," X, Nov. 10, 2023; ADL New England (@ADL_NewEngland), "Thank you President Sian Leah Beilock of @dartmouth for protecting all students' right to learn in a safe environment while upholding the value of freedom," X, May 2, 2024.

95 "We built academic infrastructures": Ghazal Golshiri, "All 12 Universities in Gaza Have Been the Target of Israeli Attacks: 'It's a War Against Education,'" *Le Monde,* March 7, 2024.

95 college students make up: "Indicators: Total Population, Gaza Strip," Palestinian Central Bureau of Statistics, www.pcbs.gov.ps. For the U.K., see Paul Bolton, "Higher Education Student Numbers," Research Briefing, House of Commons Library, researchbriefings .parliament.uk; and "Population Estimates for the UK, England, Wales, Scotland, and Northern Ireland: Mid-2021," Office for National Statistics, Dec. 21, 2022, www.ons.gov.uk.

96 "Tactics of intimidation": Anti-Defamation League (@ADL), "Finally. Thank you, @Columbia, for enforcing your policies & acting in a way consistent with your legal & moral obligations to protect Jewish students."

96 Several days earlier, Israel: Golshiri, "All 12 Universities in Gaza Have Been the Target of Israeli Attacks."

96 Videos showed its buildings: Jordan News staff, "Israel Flattens Al Azhar University in Gaza," *Jordan News,* Nov. 4, 2023.

96 according to UNESCO: "Impact on the Education Sector," UNESCO's Action in the Gaza Strip, accessed June 16, 2024, www.unesco.org.

96 "The word 'dreams'": Aaron Boxerman, Iyad Abuheweila, and Ameera Harouda, "They Graduated into Gaza's War. What Happened to Them?," *New York Times,* April 18, 2024.

96 Between them, the X accounts: Tweets were extracted from keyword searches using the Meltwater platform.

5 · KORACH'S CHILDREN

97 "All the community": Numbers 16:3.

97 "the conscience of Israel": "Yeshayahu Leibowitz," in *Stanford Encyclopedia of Philosophy,* March 29, 2011, revised March 6, 2019, plato.stanford.edu.

97 "observe all My commandments": Numbers 15:40.

98 "You alone": Amos 3:2.

98 "the prophets": Held, *Judaism Is About Love,* 339.

98 eleventh-century Spanish poet: Yeshayahu Leibowitz, "Idolatry," in *Contemporary Jewish Religious Thought: Original Essays on Critical Concepts, Movements, and Beliefs,* ed. Arthur A. Cohen and Paul Mendes-Flohr (New York: Charles Scribner's Sons, 1987), 448.

99 the Israelite elders: 1 Samuel 8:4–22.

99 In Jewish tradition: Reuven Kimmelman, "The Theology and Politics of Idolatry," in *Idolatry: A Contemporary Jewish Conversation,* ed. Alon Goshen-Gottstein (Brookline, Mass.: Academic Studies Press, 2023), 68, 132, 180.

99 to prevent Jewish Pharaohs: The Israeli philosophers Moshe Halbertal and Avishai Margalit note that an "Israelite king has no special role in divine worship." Moshe Halbertal and Avishai Margalit, *Idolatry,* trans. Naomi Goldblum (Cambridge, Mass.: Harvard University Press, 1992), 220.

99 "observe faithfully": Deuteronomy 17:19–20.

100 "judges and is judged": Babylonian Talmud, Sanhedrin 19a.

100 States are not created: As Abraham Joshua Heschel put it, "There is something in the world that the Bible does regard as a symbol of God. It is not a temple or a tree. It is not a statue or a star." Instead, "the symbol of God is the person, every person." Abraham Joshua Heschel, *The Insecurity of Freedom: Essays on Human Existence* (New York: Noonday Press, 1967), 95, cited in Held, *Judaism Is About Love,* 162. In the original, Heschel says "man" instead of "person."

101   "*Ahavat yisrael* is not": Held, *Judaism Is About Love,* 155.

101   investing supreme value: "What is an idol?" asked Heschel. "A thing, a force, a person, a group, an institution or an ideal, regarded as supreme. God alone is supreme." See Abraham Joshua Heschel, *God in Search of Man* (New York: Farrar, Straus & Cudahy, 1955), 415.

102   rejecting idolatry: Babylonian Talmud, Megillah 13a.

102   no "intrinsic value": Yeshayahu Leibowitz, "The Religious Significance of the State of Israel" (1975), in *Judaism, Human Values, and the Jewish State,* 218.

102   fourteen prime ministers: Oren Kessler, "The Meaning of Israel's First Religious Prime Minister," *Foreign Policy,* June 7, 2021.

102   "the existence of the State": A 1985 amendment to the Basic Law: The Knesset (which has constitutional status) added Section 7(A), which stipulates, "A list of candidates shall not participate in the elections for the Knesset if its aims or actions, expressly or by implication, point to one of the following: (1) denial of the existence of the State of Israel as the state of the Jewish people; (2) denial of the democratic nature of the state; and (3) incitement to racism." Amendments in 2002 changed Section 7(A)(1) to read as "denial of the existence of the State of Israel as a Jewish and democratic state" and added Section 7(A)(3), "support for armed struggle by a hostile state or a terrorist organization against the State of Israel," as an additional basis for disqualifying candidates and candidates' lists. See "Basic Law: The Knesset," Discriminatory Laws in Israel, Adalah, accessed June 26, 2024, www.adalah.org.

102   "all kinds of students": "About," Hillel International, accessed July 29, 2024, www.hillel.org.

102   "a core element": "Israel Guidelines," Hillel International, accessed July 29, 2024, www.hillel.org.

103   "the essence of fascism": Leibowitz, "Religious Significance of the State of Israel," 218.

103   "any god": Abraham Joshua Heschel, "Religion and Race," Jan. 14, 1963, voicesofdemocracy.umd.edu.

103 "in the spirit": Ibid.

103 around 6 percent: Between October 7, 2023, and September 22, 2024, at least 41,431 Palestinians were killed and 95,818 were injured in Gaza, according to the Gaza Health Ministry. See Palestinian Ministry of Health/Gaza (t.me/MOHMediaGaza), "Daily statistical report on the number of martyrs and injured as a result of the ongoing Israeli aggression on the Gaza Strip for the 352nd day" [in Arabic], Telegram, Sept. 22, 2024. The population in the Gaza Strip as of 2023 was 2,226,544, according to the Palestinian Bureau of Central Statistics. See "Indicators," Palestinian Central Bureau of Statistics. On casualty figures from the Health Ministry versus Israel's own estimates in past wars, see Isabel Debre, "What Is Gaza's Ministry of Health and How Does It Calculate the War's Death Toll?," Associated Press, Nov. 7, 2023.

103 would take eighty years: Anushka Patil, "U.N. Report Says Rebuilding All the Homes Destroyed in Gaza Could Take 80 Years," *New York Times,* May 2, 2024.

104 "Israel is creating": I. F. Stone, "Holy War," *New York Review of Books,* Aug. 3, 1967.

104 the 92nd Street Y: "James Baldwin at 92nd St. Y," *New York Times,* July 19, 1983; "Susan Sontag: 'On Classical Pornography,'" 92NY Plus, March 6, 2014, www.youtube.com/@92YPlus; Jennifer Schuessler, "92NY Halts Literary Series After Pulling Author Critical of Israel," *New York Times,* Oct. 23, 2023.

105 "feel safe": Kate Hidalgo Bellows, "A Campus Where Everyone Is Just Like You," *Chronicle of Higher Education,* Feb. 26, 2024; Ron Liebowitz, "A Space for Free Speech, Not Hate Speech," Brandeis University Office of the President, Nov. 8, 2023.

105 right-leaning Zionist Organization: The legislation defines antisemitism according to the International Holocaust Remembrance Alliance working definition, which includes among its examples "Denying the Jewish people their right to self-determination, e.g., by claiming that the existence of a State of Israel is a racist endeavor." See "Working Definition of Antisemitism," International Holocaust Remembrance Alliance, holocaustremembrance

.com. On the legislation, see "H.R. 3773—Stop Anti-Semitism on College Campuses Act," introduced by Representative Mike Lawler (R-N.Y.) on May 31, 2023, www.congress.gov. See also "ZOA Deeply Appreciates Cong. Mike Lawler & Co-sponsors for Introducing Important 'Stop Antisemitism on College Campuses Act,'" Zionist Organization of America, June 7, 2023, www.zoa .org.

105 as Donald Trump: "Jonathan Greenblatt Introduction and Jared Kushner Keynote Remarks," Never Is Now 2024, Anti-Defamation League, March 12, 2024, www.youtube.com/@Anti -Defamation-League.

105 AIPAC endorsed: Data generated based on publicly available information. See Karen Yourish, Larry Buchanan, and Denise Lu, "The 147 Republicans Who Voted to Overturn Election Results," *New York Times,* Jan. 7, 2021; "Support Pro-Israel Candidates," AIPAC Political Portal, accessed July 3, 2024, candidates .aipacpac.org.

106 contributing "to intensified antisemitism": "ADL Condemns Amnesty International's Latest Effort to Demonize Israel," Anti-Defamation League, Jan. 30, 2022, www.adl.org.

106 former head of the Mossad: Harry Davies, "Revealed: Israeli Spy Chief 'Threatened' ICC Prosecutor over War Crimes Inquiry," *Guardian,* May 28, 2024.

106 a new ICC prosecutor: "House Adopts ICC Sanctions Legislation," AIPAC, June 4, 2024, www.aipac.org.

106 "in its death throes": Agnès Callamard, "Gaza and the End of the Rules-Based Order," *Foreign Affairs,* Feb. 15, 2024.

108 dotted South Africa's landscape: Jackie Grobler, "Memories of a Lost Cause: Comparing Remembrance of the Civil War by Southerners to the Anglo-Boer War by Afrikaners," *Historia* 52, no. 2 (Nov. 2006): 208.

108 "cost 20,000 lives": Pierre Hugo, "Towards Darkness and Death: Racial Demonology in South Africa," *Journal of Modern African Studies* 26, no. 4 (Dec. 1988): 581.

109 It was designated: Robert Windrem, "US Government Considered Nelson Mandela a Terrorist Until 2008," *NBC News,* Dec. 7, 2013.

109 "one settler, one bullet": Heribert Adam and Kogila Moodley, *The Opening of the Apartheid Mind: Options for the New South Africa* (Berkeley: University of California Press, 1993), 177; Donald G. McNeil Jr., "Nationalist Group Fights for Identity in South Africa," *New York Times,* May 30, 1999.

109 Even Blacks who: Seidman, "Guerrillas in Their Midst," 120.

109 "physical safety of whites": Hugo, "Towards Darkness and Death," 585.

109 "racial integration with national suicide": Allister Sparks, *Tomorrow Is Another Country: The Inside Story of South Africa's Road to Change* (New York: Hill and Wang, 1995), 8.

110 they waved banners: Donald Harman Akenson, *God's Peoples: Covenant and Land in South Africa, Israel, and Ulster* (Ithaca, N.Y.: Cornell University Press, 1992), 139–41; Owen Bowcott, "How Lies About Irish 'Barbarism' in 1641 Paved Way for Cromwell's Atrocities," *Guardian,* Feb. 18, 2011.

110 "straightforward tribal barbarism": Mark Hayes, "The Evolution of Republican Strategy and the 'Peace Process' in Ireland," *Race & Class* 39, no. 3 (1998): 25.

110 "prelude to genocide": Susan McKay, *Bear in Mind These Dead* (London: Faber and Faber, 2008), 164, cited in Colin Coulter et al., *Northern Ireland a Generation After Good Friday: Lost Futures and New Horizons in the "Long Peace"* (Manchester, UK: Manchester University Press, 2021), 34.

111 "South was set upon": George Wallace, "Segregation Now, Segregation Forever," 1963, published by BlackPast on Jan. 22, 2013, www.blackpast.org.

111 "white supremacy or black supremacy": Jason Sokol, *There Goes My Everything: White Southerners in the Age of Civil Rights, 1945–1975* (New York: Vintage Books, 2007), 80.

112 "With our boxes": Jason Burke, "Winnie Madikizela-Mandela Dies Aged 81," *Guardian,* April 2, 2018.

112 "once a nonviolent way": Mahmood Mamdani, *Good Muslim, Bad Muslim: America, the Cold War, and the Roots of Terror* (New York: Pantheon Books, 2004), 226–27.

112 instances of ethnic conflict: Lars-Erik Cederman, Andreas Wimmer, and Brian Min, "Why Do Ethnic Groups Rebel? New Data and Analysis," *World Politics* 62, no. 1 (Jan. 2010): 106.

112 "political exclusion": Limor Yehuda, *Collective Equality: Human Rights and Democracy in Ethno-national Conflicts* (Cambridge, U.K.: Cambridge University Press, 2023), 245.

113 Palestinian citizens: Raphaëlle Rérolle, "At Haifa's Hospital, Jews and Arabs Work Together in a Fragile Coexistence," *Le Monde*, Nov. 21, 2023.

113 South Africa waged war: The five are Angola, Botswana, Rhodesia/Zimbabwe, Mozambique, and Zambia. See Rodney Warwick, "Operation Savannah: A Measure of SADF Decline, Resourcefulness, and Modernisation," *Scientia Militaria* 40, no. 3 (2012): 354–97; Ian van der Waag and Albert Grundlingh, "South Africa's Border War in Retrospect," in *In Different Times: The War for Southern Africa, 1966–1989* (Stellenbosch, ZA: Sun Press, 2019); United Press International, "S. Africa Raid in Botswana Kills 13; U.S. Recalls Envoy," *Los Angeles Times*, June 16, 1985; J. R. T. Wood, *Counter-strike from the Sky: The Rhodesian All-Arms Fireforce in the War in the Bush, 1974–1980* (Newlands, ZA: 30° South Publishers, 2009); Hilton Hamann, *Days of the Generals: The Untold Story of South Africa's Apartheid-Era Military Generals* (Cape Town: Zebra Press, 2001); Leopold Scholtz, *The SADF in the Border War, 1966–1989* (Cape Town: Tafelberg, 2013).

114 a "just solution": Akiva Eldar, "Israel Ignores Iran's Support of Arab Peace Initiative," *Al-Monitor*, Dec. 31, 2017; "The Arab Peace Initiative, 2002," official translation of the full text of a Saudi-inspired peace plan adopted by the Arab summit in Beirut, 2002, www.kas.de.a13730828279&groupId=268421.

114 Northern Ireland's schools: Robin Sheeran, "Why Northern Ireland's Schools Are Still Segregated," *New Humanist*, Dec. 1, 2023.

114 Democratic political systems: Jason Burke, "Jacob Zuma Sought

to Hand State Assets to Allies, Finds Corruption Report," *Guardian,* May 1, 2022.

115 Historical wrongs: This was the theme of an essay I wrote about Palestinian refugee return in 2021. See Peter Beinart, "Teshuvah: A Jewish Case for Palestinian Refugee Return," *Jewish Currents,* May 11, 2021.

115 "Many white Southerners": Sokol, *There Goes My Everything,* 316.

116 a woman named Linda: On Linda Ervine's Irish-language school in East Belfast, see turasbelfast.com. On Protestant hostility to the Irish language in Northern Ireland, see Gordon McCoy, "Protestants and the Irish Language in Northern Ireland" (PhD diss., Queen's University Belfast, 1997). On the expulsion of Catholics from East Belfast, see SeaanUiNeill, "The Belfast Shipyard Expulsions and Their Aftermath, 21st July 1920," *Slugger O'Toole,* July 19, 2020.

116 In an interview: Rory Carroll, "'It Can't Be Sidelined': Bill Aims to Give Irish Official Status in Northern Ireland," *Guardian,* May 25, 2022.

116 "I am an African": "Statement of Deputy President Thabo Mbeki, on Behalf of the African National Congress, on the Occasion of the Adoption of the Constitutional Assembly of 'The Republic of South Africa Constitution Bill 1996': Cape Town, May 8, 1996," justice.gov.za.

116 "the African bit": John Carlin, "INTERVIEW / Young Verwoerd Is Wrestling with Sins of the Grandfather: The Grandson of Apartheid's Architect Has Joined the ANC. John Carlin Talks to Him," *Independent,* April 3, 1993.

118 "Proclaim release throughout": Leviticus 25:10.

118 A commentary attributed: Although often attributed to Falk's book, *Pnei Yehoshua,* this passage does not appear in the text, and the syntax suggests it may come from an unknown later author.

118 "One who acquires": Babylonian Talmud, Kiddushin 20a.

118 freeing the oppressed: According to a more straightforward reading, the verse refers to "inhabitants" in general and not "slaves"

in particular because the Jubilee also involves the cancellation of debts and the return of ancestral holdings. The commentary attributed to Falk is creatively reinterpreting the verse.

120 "We, with love": James Baldwin, *The Fire Next Time* (London: Michael Joseph, 1963), 21.

120 South Africa's legal team: Narnia Bohler-Muller, "South Africa's Legal Team in the Genocide Case Against Israel Has Won Praise. Who Are They?," *Conversation,* Jan. 12, 2024; "Sarah Pudfin-Jones," Ubunye Chambers, Members, accessed July 25, 2024.

121 "All the families": Genesis 12:3.

A NOTE ABOUT THE AUTHOR

Peter Beinart is professor of journalism and political science at the Craig Newmark Graduate School of Journalism at the City University of New York. He is also editor at large of *Jewish Currents,* a contributing opinion writer at *The New York Times,* an MSNBC political commentator, and a nonresident fellow at the Foundation for Middle East Peace. He writes the *Beinart Notebook* newsletter on Substack.com. He lives in New York with his family.

A NOTE ON THE TYPE

This book was set in Minion, a typeface produced by the Adobe Corporation specifically for the Macintosh personal computer and released in 1990. Designed by Robert Slimbach, Minion combines the classic characteristics of old-style faces with the full complement of weights required for modern typesetting.

Typeset by Scribe,
Philadelphia, Pennsylvania

Printed and bound by Berryville Graphics,
Berryville, Virginia

Designed by Cassandra J. Pappas